Don Ma

THE 12 HIDDEN LAWS OF PERFORMANCE

How to use your mind to win in sport and life

www.the12lawsofperformance.co

TABLE OF CONTENTS

I

Foreword

Are you a champion?
Would you like to be?

Athletic performance is perhaps the ultimate proving ground for psychological insight. Day after day, in gyms, training grounds, and stadiums around the world, people put their minds and bodies on the line in pursuit of perfection. Where an idea comes from isn't important; the only question any athlete worth their salt asks is "Does it work?"

The book you are about to read works. It is an elegant blending of ancient wisdom, inspiring stories and cutting edge psychological practice. But more than that, it's a guidebook you can use on your journey to success in sport and in life. As Don McNaughton, a top performance coach to real-life champions points out , you do need the physical skills to succeed in your chosen field of endeavor. But more than that, you must have 'the mental skill to allow yourself to do what you know you are physically capable of doing.'

In working with Don over the past few years, I have been continually impressed by the way he is able to use cutting edge mind technology with a simplicity that works for everyone from an Olympic athlete to an elite footballer to a group of teenagers trying to find their way in the world. What's even more impressive is that you can absorb so much of that wisdom through the pages that follow.

This book won't give you the physical skills it takes to succeed. No book can. But what it can give you is even more important, because it is within your control – the mental skills, inspiration and understanding that fuel the physical actions that turn failure into success and winners into champions. Read this book, enjoy the stories and reflect on the laws of success. Then go out into the arena and apply what you have learned. The life you change may be your own!

Michael Neill, internationally renowned success coach and author of *You Can Have What You Want, Supercoach* and *Effortless Success*
www.supercoach.com; http://www.supercoach.com

Praise for Don MacNaughton

'I have got to know Don MacNaughton very well over the two years he has helped me at Inverness Caledonian Thistle FC. He has helped to transform the club during this period following its relegation and promotion in successive years. His techniques are simple but extremely effective and the players have all come to admire and respect his intuitive and instructive manner. Don can easily teach and improve large or small groups but is inspirational on a one to one basis; with any sporting pursuit. I have no hesitation in recommending anyone to employ Don MacNaughton - it would be a massive step in securing a brighter and more satisfying future.'

Terry Butcher, Manager Inverness Caledonian Thistle F.C.

'Don has impressed me with his understanding of what matters in sports performance. Mental skills are the decisive factor in what makes an athlete successful, and he knows how to present and implement this training the right way. I'm looking forward to using the 12 laws with our athletes.'

Sacha Van Der Most, Head of Youth Development Chivas USA

'After knowing Don for seven years I have come to recognize his passion for helping individuals reach their very best. He shares this information with everyone by pinpointing the invisible habits necessary to construct an effective, winning mind-set.'

Tonya Reiman author of 'The Yes Factor'

'In today's world cutting through the crap and noise of what works is the key to performance success. Don offers us simple, profound and effective laws that will if followed raise your performance.'

Andrea J. Lee, CEO, Thought Partners International
http://www.wealthythoughtleader.com

'Don MacNaughton delivers the hidden keys to internal personal commitment and mental motivation in this straightforward, hard-hitting book that reveals the workings of a successful athlete's mind.'

Steve Chandler Author of 'Time Warrior'

'I have been working as a sports psychologist for over 35 years and have written and published 10 books on the subject . I have had the honor and privilege of working with Don MacNaughton many times and I must say that his genuine,authentic and knowledgeable understanding of the material in his book as well as his ability to deliver it's essence in his work is remarkable. I intend to keep this wonderful book by my side as a handy quick reference to helping me to help my athletes succeed. If the mental game is what you are after, you must read this book.'

Dr. Jerry Lynch Author of 'Thinking Body, Dancing Mind' and 'The Way of the Champion'

'When it comes to working with athletes, no one is better than Don MacNaughton. He has a way of cutting through all extraneous thought to get to the essence of what it takes to maximize performance. His results prove it. Not only that, the "laws" he works with apply not only to athletes but to everyone in daily life.'

Jack Pransky, Ph.D Author of 'Somebody Should Have Told Us!: Simple Truths for Living Well'

If you want to raise your game you need to understand the mental process that great performers use which you will find in The 12 Hidden Laws. Who better than author Don MacNaughton who has coached the world's leading sports and business people to win.

Robbie Stenhouse Author of " How to coach with NLP"

"The inspirational stories in Don's book are backed up with tried and tested techniques that anyone can use to take their performance to a whole new level.

I have been using Don's relaxation and visualisation techniques for over 10 years and in challenging situations they have always delivered incredible results. In 2006 I was in the final of the JCI World Public Speaking Championships and used Don's relaxation anchors to deal with incredible pressure and win the competition. Read the book, apply the principles and enjoy a lifetime of successful results"

Andy McKechnie Junior Chamber International 2006 World Public Speaking Champion

"Don has helped me to become mentally stronger and more balanced and consistent in my mental preparation, even in high stress situations. He has taught me to avoid negative thoughts and form positive images, taking positive lessons from all situations"

Ben Kilner (GB World Cup snowboarder)

By combining cutting edge principles of modern sports coaching together with a remarkable understanding of the Natural Laws, Don has given us a powerful aid to take control of our progression. This book can be used as a personal guide or as a useful coaching resource. The fusion of modern and ancient principles provides a firm root while also eliciting power inspiration.

Tony Felix - Martial Arts champion. International Martial Arts Coach, Personal Trainer, NLP Master Practitioner and Life Coach.

"Don MacNaughton bypasses the modern fixation on "adopting winning mindsets" and instead gives the reader the freedom to build his own. This happens through the introduction of twelve simple yet powerful laws: conditions which determine success. By understanding the unshakable framework of what it takes to succeed, the book then guides its reader to understand his own internal dialogue, external relationships, support structures - building mindsets which support goals at a more personal level. In this way, MacNaughton sheds motivational instruction in favor of a more visceral, personal and accomplishable model."

Ian Bryan
President & Founder Sensible City

"Us Scottish folk don't mince our words with one another, we say it how it is. Here's how it is; Don's absolutely the real deal, straight to the point and totally authentic and his book is too... Buy it!'

Ali Campbell author of "Just Get On with It"

Don takes sports psychology theory and transforms it into an effective skillset anybody can put to work for greater performance!"

Eric Black First Team Coach Sunderland AFC

The Story Behind the Author and the Book

Who is Don MacNaughton and why should you listen to a guy from the Highlands of Scotland about performance?

In the part of the world which I come from it is frowned upon to say what you are good at, or stick your head above the parapet but I cannot keep what I know undercover any more. So here's a little bit about my journey and how the 12 Laws turned my life around.

Above my desk I keep a picture of a little boy of four kicking a big football on the beach in Northumberland, England with his Dad.

The boy in the picture is me.

We are all given clues in our life of the places where we come alive and the places where we really live. Life has a way of leaving a trail and the picture above my desk is a part of mine.

My journey began in a little Scottish Highland village called Brora in Sutherland. Growing up there offered me opportunities to play, to grow and to explore and I loved sport, especially football, tennis and badminton. Those were the days when I would go out with my mates and kick a football around until we could no longer see in the dark - and even then we'd still try to keep playing! It didn't matter if we lost track of time because our mums would call us in; I now know this to be termed as being in the flow state but more on that later.

My mum also loved sport and encouraged me to play. She was a really good tennis player and I learned through her how great it is to have someone who encourages you 'on your team'.

My dad took me to my first big football game when I was nine years old; Glasgow Celtic vs. Hibernian. I had never seen so many people in one place and I had never experienced an atmosphere like it. Celtic won 6-1 and I felt sure I wanted to be a footballer and play for the famous Glasgow Celtic.

I loved to play football, as many young boys do, but to become a professional would require something more; I would need discipline, focus and a growth mindset, all subjects covered in detail in the following chapters.

When I was just 11 years old, my dad died after a long illness and my life was thrown into disarray. A happy-go-lucky kid turned into a surly, angry boy with a chip on his shoulder. How we deal with the challenges of life is important and we should always remember that everyone does the best they can with the resources they have at the time. At the age of 11, all I thought I had was my anger! I put my poor mum through a lot but she taught me the power of love and acceptance, and that even they can't guarantee instant results.

Teenage years can be such defining times in a young person's life. I recently bumped into my old gym teacher Willie MacKay and I was able to tell him what sport has given me in my life; from my perspective, more than any other skill set and more than I learned academically in school or at university. Through my love of sport I have also been able to make friends and travel the world, speaking the universal language of football.

The ability to set goals, fall down, get back up again, and work as a team - all learned through sport. Through working with top professionals in sport, I have learned what it takes to make it to the top of your game and to realise your true potential. The lessons learned through the experiences of those top players are lessons that have helped me to realise my own success and I can now share them with you in this book.

Life can sometimes take you in unexpected directions and things don't always go according to plan. I was involved in a car accident that I was lucky to escape without serious physical injury but which triggered a chain of events that led me away from sport and had a negative effect on my life. Being able to go back to that little boy on the beach held the key to being able to change my life as I was able to reconnect with my love of sport.

From there, I was able to see where my skills overlapped with my passions and this allowed me to recognise new opportunities and, with a bit of work, those opportunities increased and kept coming. In the eight years from starting my performance consulting business, Zoned In Performance, I've gone from having zero clients and earning only £100 per week from working in a tennis club to travelling the world and working with international teams and some of the biggest names in sport.

This is not something that happened by 'magic' but by being aligned with who I am and working hard on my skills. I think it's fair to say that anyone who met me 20 years ago would struggle to believe that I've achieved all that I have today because, not putting too fine a point on it, I was not one of life's shining diamonds and it would have been difficult to even recognise the diamond in the rough within me. Everyone has the potential to change and I know for certain that anything is possible when you are open to embracing that change.

This book shares with you the 12 Hidden Laws of Performance that you can use to achieve your dreams and realise your goals in sport and life. I have used "superstar" illustrations within the book but in my everyday life and business encounters, I help people who have not yet hit the back page. Many of my clients are now good friends and they are great examples of 'ordinary' people who have taken amazing steps to achieve their goals. One such person is Joe, a young soccer player. His story highlights that when we choose our attitude, amazing things can happen and life opens up. Joe was a boy with amazing talent and, like most of us, his challenge was to allow that talent to shine. Joe had effectively shut his future opportunities down through the emotional lens that he was carrying around. He was so caught up with the 'if' in life that he thought in terms of, "If I get a run in the first team then I will have a good attitude" instead of thinking in terms of developing a good attitude first! There are no guarantees but Joe learned that he must apply himself as if he was a first team player and train as if he was already a first team player in order to become that first team player. The next day he was playing in front of a crowd of 30 people and unbeknown to him the manager was one of those watching him. He was impressed by what he saw and immediately put Joe into the first team squad for the game the next day.

On the day of the game, Joe came out on to the pitch to play in front of a crowd of 58, 000 people - as the song lyrics say, what a difference a day makes! When you learn to recognise and then choose your attitude, you learn to recognise the opportunities that are all around you and you learn to choose the ones that are right for you. Opportunities are everywhere and they are yours for the taking, you just have to take steps to ensure you're not shutting yourself off from them.

Most people think that I am 'lucky' and perhaps that's true. What I know for sure is that I have worked hard on the skills and attitudes I know will allow me to develop as a person and as a coach. I don't live my life by luck, I live my life by being the best I can be. In this book I will show you how to do the same.

Acknowledgments

With grateful thanks to my coaches, teachers and sponsors Robert Dilts, Steve Chandler, Michael Neill, Jack Pransky and Alistair Macpherson who have made a monumental difference to my coaching and to myself.

My sports coaches Alfie Abbott and Willie Mackay who didn't see an awkward, argumentative child, but the potential to be something better.

To the team; Linda and James who made this book spring to life.

And of course my beautiful wife, Freyja and son Jack for loving and teaching me there is "more to life" and living fully in the present is to win in life.

Dedicated to my Mam, Jean MacNaughton, who I miss every day.

28/4/25 to 10/7/10

" It is only with the heart that one can see rightly; what is essential is invisible to the eye"

Antoine de Saint-Exupéry

Introduction

Sports psychology only became a recognised science in the 1920s but its origins can be traced back to the 'healthy mind, healthy body' philosophy of Ancient Greek and Chinese civilisations. Many of the guiding principles known as the Laws of the Universe also have origins dating back centuries but it was not until the early 1900s that books on the subject began to bring the principles to a wider audience. However, the more we learn about them, the more we come to realise that the Laws have always been in existence and always will be in existence, regardless of whether we are aware of them or not.

The Laws of the Universe are described as guidelines that can enhance our physical, mental, emotional and spiritual growth, allowing us to live fully and realise our true potential in whatever we choose to do. Mental skills training is recognised today as playing a key role in helping competitive athletes to achieve their full potential in sport and the techniques used to enhance sporting performance are now also used to equally great affect in other areas of life. Neuro-Linguistic Programming (NLP) began as a study of successful language patterns in the 1970s and has since developed into a study of effective behavioural patterns alongside language. In brief, 'neuro' relates to how we use our bodies; 'linguistic' relates to how we use language and how we communicate; and 'programming' relates to the maps we make and the strategies we use in our brain. At its core, NLP is a study of what makes successful people successful and is used in sport as a powerful method of discovering how top athletes produce excellence in their performances.

The basic principle behind the Laws of the Universe, also known as the Laws of Nature, is that everything in the universe is energy and our thoughts, feelings, words, and actions are no exception. Everything we think, feel, say, and do is responsible for our reality so, in other words, your emotional state has a direct effect on your physical state. The key lesson that all of us can learn through an understanding of the Universal Laws is that we all have the capacity to change our circumstances in life by changing our mental attitude to them and by learning how to use the natural flow of energy that exists all around us to create the world we want.

In sport, it's now widely recognised that champions become champions from within, and the key to realising a top performance is to develop mental skill alongside physical skill. The connection between the Universal Laws and sports performance is therefore the phenomenal power of the mind and by applying ancient wisdom to modern sport, a powerful new way of thinking about improving sports performance emerges.

Law One

A Top Performance Is An Inspired Performance

Find Your Passion

"To succeed…You need to find something to hold on to, something to motivate you, something to inspire you"

- Tony Dorsett, American football running back

A great many successful sportspeople have been described as 'inspired athletes' or 'inspired players' and their achievements described as 'inspired' performances, so what makes them inspired? What's the source of that inspiration?

It's a Universal Law that we're all connected: we live in a world where everything is connected to everything else, including us. Everything we do, say, think, and believe affects others and the universe around us. In other words, we all have the capacity to both inspire others and be inspired by others.

CHAMPIONS ARE MADE, NOT BORN.

So who or what inspires the 'inspired': who or what makes the sports champions? Behind every successful athlete there's a successful support team who all play an important role in inspiring the success of the athlete they support. They might be a physiotherapist, a nutritionist, a sports psychologist, a fitness trainer or a coach but they are all inspired to do what they do and to do it to the best of their ability in order to allow those they support to achieve *their* full potential. They are all inspired performers: they are *all* passionate about what they do.

Each and every one of us has within us our own source of inspiration as we are all inspired by the things we feel passionate about. A coach who is passionate about their sport instils that passion into everyone around them: an inspired coach can inspire every athlete they connect with at every level of their sport. They may not be the champion athlete's coach on the day that they become champion but they may well have inspired that athlete on their journey to the top of their sport. Athletes who become champions often attribute their success to the coaches who inspired them at each stage in their career, so who or what inspires the coaches?

Successful coaches are undoubtedly inspired by other successful coaches just as successful athletes are inspired by the success of other athletes. Neuro-Linguistic Programming (NLP) is, in a nutshell, a study of what makes successful people successful and at its core, it's simply a method of discovering how *anyone* produces excellence in *anything*. NLP is now widely used in sport, in business, in education, and in general by anyone interested in developing better personal effectiveness in life. NLP sport focuses specifically on the success of sportspeople but the common link across all areas is that NLP is a way of discovering how to be the best *you* can be in whatever it is *you* do.

NLP encourages curiosity. It encourages everyone to be curious about themselves, curious about other people, and curious about the world they live in. Through NLP, you become aware of the connections that already exist between you and those you study and you gain an understanding of how you see the world and how you think. Crucially, you also learn to question your views. Do the successful people you aspire to be see and think the way you do? Is it possible that your current beliefs and behavioural patterns could be holding you back?

What began as a study of successful language patterns back in the 1970s, developed rapidly into a study of effective behavioural patterns, encompassing not only the language used by successful people but also the routine thought processes, emotions, and actions of high achievers. NLP sports models of excellence are inspirational role models but NLP promotes the importance and the value of maintaining your own individual uniqueness. Much can be learned from following the training schedule of a successful athlete or from eating the same diet but to really learn the secret of their success, you need to understand how they connect with the world and the people around them on a daily basis. You need an understanding of their routine 'habits' - how do they view life; how do they respond physically and emotionally to everyday challenges?

INSPIRED CONNECTIONS

When good athletes become *great* athletes, people always want to know who inspired them. Most successful people model themselves on inspirational characters and sport is no exception. In the 2002 Salt Lake City winter Olympics, Jim Shea of the USA won gold in the skeleton. In the 1964 Innsbruck games, his father Jim Shea Sr. was a member of the US ski team and his grandfather, Jack Shea, won two speed skating gold medals in the Lake Placid games in1932. It would seem that Jim Shea Jr. only had to look to his family for inspiration.

So who or what inspired Jack Shea to become a double-gold medal winner back in 1932? He didn't have an immediate family connection to the sport. Perhaps it was fellow American Charles Jewtraw who won the first speed skating event in the first ever winter Olympics held at Chamonix in 1924. Jewtraw's win caused an upset in a sport normally dominated by Scandinavians so where did *his* inspiration come from? Perhaps Shea's inspiration came from Finnish speed skater Clas Thunberg who won an awe inspiring three gold medals in 1932. Of course, he may not have been inspired by anyone or anything to do with his sport but he would no doubt still be aware of influential characters in his life who helped him to achieve his dream.

'The ripple of influence' is a term used to describe the ripple effect an inspirational coach can have on the lives of others. Just as one pebble dropped into a pond will create a great many ripples that spread out across the water, a coach may influence and inspire a great many people beyond those they coach.

Many young athletes are both influenced and inspired by their coaches. Figure skating champion Sonja Henie of Norway was only fifteen years of age when she won her first Olympic gold medal in 1928. She went on to win a further two golds, matching the record set by her coach Gillis Grafstrom of Sweden who won his third consecutive gold medal at St. Moritz in 1928.

Using a sports hero as a role model allows us to study what they say, what they think, what they feel, and what they do. To become successful ourselves, we have to understand the 'habits' of successful people. Henie no doubt observed the habits of her coach and Shea Jr. no doubt picked up the habits of his father and grandfather. Studying the habits of successful people you admire or inspirational people in your life can open your mind to the potential for achieving more.

CONNECT WITH YOUR PASSION AND YOUR TRUE SELF TO FIND YOUR INSPIRATION.

Everyone has the potential to change and everyone has the potential to be excellent in whatever they put their mind to. What *you* put your mind to is what inspires *you*. Inspired sportspeople put their minds' into only what's important, their sport. Sport is their passion.

It takes a clear understanding of who you are now and where you are now to be able to move forward and get to where you want to be. People change, situations change, and the world we live in is constantly changing so it's important to continue questioning whether your own beliefs and attitudes have changed accordingly. Through NLP, it becomes possible to identify the changes you need to make and to be open to the positive benefits that making those changes could bring. Effectively, NLP is a study of how to be a better you, in everything you do.

Strong Connections

A successful sports team is much more than a group of inspired players, it's a group of players who are all connected by team spirit.

Team Spirit = a creative energy found in teams who have greater strength and ability as a unit compared to as individuals.

A successful team coach develops a successful team by observing the principles of this 'all for one and one for all' inspired Law of performance and promoting team spirit. We only have to look back at England's performance in the 2010 FIFA World Cup to see a good example of the negative effects of the 'every man for himself' attitude in team sports. The England squad was comprised of the cream of English soccer players but, clearly, a group of talented individuals doesn't necessarily create a talented team.

Jim Loehr is a world-renowned performance psychologist. He says, "Full engagement is the pathway to extraordinary performance," and in relation to team sports he adds, "Players who are fully engaged bring their best energy to the team." So, what does it mean to be "fully engaged" and where can a player's "best energy" be sourced?

THE MISSING LINK BETWEEN 'EVERY MAN FOR HIMSELF' AND 'ONE FOR ALL' IS TEAM SPIRIT.

Team spirit is the source of a team's creative energy and team spirit is also the source of a player's 'best energy'. Best energy is inspired energy; positive energy that creates the will to win. If a player has the will to win, they are fully focused on playing their best and on doing their bit to allow the team to achieve a best performance: they are 'fully engaged'.

"There are plenty of teams in every sport that have great players and never win titles. Most of the time, those players aren't willing to sacrifice

> *for the greater good of the team. The funny thing is, in the end, their unwillingness to sacrifice only makes individual goals more difficult to achieve. One thing I believe to the fullest is that if you think and achieve as a team, the individual accolades will take care of themselves. Talent wins games, but teamwork and intelligence win championships"*
> **- Michael Jordan, basketball legend**

Team spirit is something that can develop naturally among players who spend a lot of time together in training as well as in competition but an inspired team coach can also inspire team spirit in his players by promoting team meetings and encouraging open, honest lines of communication. **England's perceived lack of team spirit in the World Cup drew attention to the fact that providing the appropriate environment and opportunities for a team to bond is an essential element of competitive team sport preparation. And, the culture within the team may ultimately have led to a lack of connection between the players and the manager. A positive team environment is essential if team spirit is to develop and the positive vibe generated by a team of connected players becomes what is essentially a key aspect of the 'invisible architecture of success'.** As team manager Fabio Capello discovered, bringing together of a group of world class players does not guarantee you a world class team!

INSPIRATIONAL SPEECHES - INSPIRE AND BE INSPIRED

Dedicate Your Game
(American football locker-room speech)
Most of you have been playing football for a good number of years now. I want you to take a moment, take a quiet moment to yourself now, and think about all the people who have helped you in your football journey

through the years. Think of all those people who have influenced you… your parents, siblings, and family; your different coaches, your teachers, your friends, neighbours, and relatives; the people in the community, the fans, and the supporters. Take this time to remember all of them.

Remember the coach who taught you how to tackle for the first time. Remember the others who played with you and against you to make you who you are today. Remember the fans and supporters who raised monies to fund your equipment through the years. Remember the adult who played catch with you after you learned to walk. Remember the family member who encouraged you to go on when you wanted to quit. Remember your parents who bought your shoes, your Under Armour®, and dropped everything to take you to practices and attend your games. Take this time to remember all of them.

Now, I want you to pick one person, one special person who in your mind sticks out above the rest. Someone who has helped you more than the others. That person who is most responsible for you being here in this locker-room today. You are going to dedicate your performance today to them. This is your day to honour them, to repay them for all that they sacrificed for you.

Keep that person in your thoughts as you go all out in each and every play, so that when the final whistle blows, you will be satisfied that you honoured them with a total sacrifice of yourself…from your mind and from your body.

Let's get it done!

- Mike Sellers, PreGameSpeeches.com

Ancient Way to Modern Day

In 1897, Norman Triplett, a psychologist from Indiana University was the first researcher to confirm that cyclists, in the majority of cases, rode faster when they cycled in groups or in pairs compared to when they cycled alone. In 1898, he became the first doctor recognised for publishing an article on social facilitation: how the presence of coaches or other athletes enhances arousal in sport.

In 1920, Dr Carl Diem, creator of the traditional torch relay in today's modern Olympics, opened the first dedicated sports psychology laboratory in Berlin and in 1923, Dr Coleman Griffith offered the first course in sports psychology at the University of Illinois in the USA. Griffith led extensive research into the psychological factors that affect sports performance and published two books, The Psychology of Coaching in 1926 and The Psychology of Athletes in 1928.

Triplett's early research led to further studies and the results of each new era of research continued to lead to a greater understanding of what had gone before. We can all learn from the experiences of others and it's a message that has been passed down through centuries of sayings and proverbs. An ancient Chinese saying is;

A bridge is not built from one piece of wood.

The way to the top in sport is to seek out those who can help you and accept all offers of help that will support you on your journey to success.

Law Two

Positive Thoughts Generate Positive Outcomes

Create Your Own Positive Vibe

"The mind is the limit. As long as the mind can envision the fact that you can do something, you can do it, as long as you really believe 100 percent"

- **Arnold Schwarzenegger**

Have you ever had a 'good feeling' about something? A feeling that lets you know that whatever it is you're doing is the right thing for you and it's the right time for you to be doing it. What is that feeling: how do you define a 'good feeling'?

Let's say you're a three-day-event rider. You're out on the course on the cross-country element and you're approaching a difficult combination fence that has two options. One option is technically more challenging than the other with the most challenging option representing the quickest but 'riskiest' route through and the less challenging option representing a 'safer' but slower route. You're riding against the clock and will incur time penalties if you fail to complete the course within the time limit but the more technically challenging an obstacle is, the greater the potential to accumulate penalties through a refusal or even a fall - which option do you choose? The answer is, you choose the option that 'feels' right. So what creates that feeling?

It's a Universal Law that *everything* creates a vibration. Everything in the universe is simply energy and is therefore in constant motion, including us. We're all familiar with the concept of generating physical vibrations but it takes a deeper  understanding of the Law of Vibration to realise that we also generate mental vibrations. Every thought, every emotion and every feeling we have creates its own unique vibration in the universe. You can't always see things moving or vibrating but you can still recognise that they are. For example, when you're standing still, you're not physically moving but you're able to understand that there are a huge number of muscles contracting and relaxing to keep you standing still. Your body is in a constant state of motion.

EVERYTHING IS ENERGY, EVERYTHING VIBRATES.

This is a concept that can be better understood through scientific research and a study of how an EEG (electroencephalograph) can read the electrical activity of the brain or how an ECG (electrocardiograph) can read the electrical charges of heart contractions but for the purposes of this book, it's going to be left as one of those things that 'just is'! It's not a difficult concept to accept when you think of it in terms of being able to 'feel' an atmosphere. Ever walked into a sports arena and felt an 'electric' atmosphere? Ever walked into a room and felt a 'bad' atmosphere, even though no-one was actually saying or doing anything to openly suggest hostility? That good or bad vibe that you've experienced is all down to vibrating energy.

So, getting back to choosing the option that 'feels' right out on the cross-country course. The 'feeling' you pick up on is the vibrating energy that's present all around you. Good vibrations are simply positive energy but here's the thing, it's energy that is being generated by *you*. The option that 'feels' right is the option that you choose to think most positively about. Your positive thoughts create positive energy and when you put positive energy out into the universe you attract positive outcomes in return. Think of it a bit like a battery; positive thoughts charge up the energy supply and negative thoughts deplete it. The Universal Law of Vibration is inextricably linked to the Law of Attraction, a concept explained later in **Law Seven**, but for now, the fact that positive thoughts lead to positive actions which, in turn, leads to positive outcomes is the key message.

A GOOD VIBE IS THE RETURN OF POSITIVE ENERGY GENERATED BY YOU.

When you *think* positively, you act positively. In this case, your positive thoughts are fuelled by the positive energy being generated by *everything* positive in your immediate environment. This will be a combination of how your ride has gone so far; how confident, secure, and in control you are feeling as the rider in the saddle; how successfully you've negotiated the previous fences and, of course, how confidently your horse is performing. You 'sense' the energy. All of your senses are guiding you - what you're thinking, what you're feeling, what you're seeing, and what you're hearing at that precise moment in time.

In **Law One**, you learned that everything is connected to everything else and everything you do, say, think, and believe affects other people and other things. Out on the cross-country course, your thoughts and actions directly affect the thoughts and actions of your horse, and vice-versa. If you send out positive energy, your horse senses that energy and responds positively. When your horse is sending out positive energy, you sense that energy and respond positively. The end result is an atmosphere 'charged' with positive energy or 'best energy' and it's best energy that creates the will to win - the will to give whatever it is you're doing your best shot.

Positive energy   →   focused actions   →   positive results

When you feel an electric atmosphere at a sporting event, you're feeling the positive energy being sent out by everyone present. When you feel a bad atmosphere in a room, you're feeling the negative energy being sent out by everyone present. So here's a thought; what if you're the only one present? Where does that good or bad vibe come from? The answer is, it comes from you. All of your senses generate their own unique vibrations so your own thoughts, words, actions, and beliefs are responsible for the vibe you feel when you're alone. If you're sending out positive energy by thinking positively, you attract positive energy in return. Positive energy brings positive things into your life; it manifests itself as the things you're focusing on achieving. But, if you're sending out negative energy by thinking negatively, you can only attract negative energy in return. If you're focusing only on the negative, only negative things can come into your life.

Let's go back out onto the cross-country course. You're approaching the combination fence feeling positive that the quickest route is the best option. You have a 'good feeling' about it, you believe in your own ability and the ability of your horse, you commit to your choice and you go for it. Result - you're through safely and on your way to the next obstacle, feeling positively charged and on a roll. However, if you're approaching the same fence feeling unsure of which option to take, doubting your ability to tackle the quickest route and stressing over time penalties if you opt for the 'safer' route, you're thinking negatively and you're not committed to either option. Result - your horse feels the negative energy of your uncertainty and slams on the brakes in front of the fence!

> *"To achieve great things, you have first to believe it"*
> **- Arsene Wenger, football manager**

THE POWER OF THE MIND

All vibrations have their own frequency and the vibrations generated by your thoughts are no exception. When you learn to harness the power of your mind, you learn that the higher frequency of positive thoughts can effectively cancel out the lower frequency of negative thoughts.

Austrian downhill skier Franz Klammer not only understood the power of his mind, he understood the phenomenal power of positive thinking. In the 1976 Innsbruck winter Olympics, Klammer was odds-on favourite to win gold. Having already won numerous races on the World Cup circuit, three of them in that year, he was a huge star and enormously popular with the home crowd in Innsbruck. On the day of the race, 60 000 screaming spectators lined the course to cheer on their hero - that's a lot of positive energy! It then transpired that Klammer would ski 15th out of a 15-man seeding: the crowd were audibly disappointed. They believed that his chance of gold was all but lost because snow conditions were such that the course would be a vertical skating rink by then. The positive vibe the crowd had been generating became a 60 000 person strong negative vibe in an instant.

Klammer *must* have felt the change of energy in the atmosphere but if he had chosen to adopt the attitude of the crowd that day, there would have been little point in competing at all. If negative thoughts had entered his head then yes, he *would* already have lost his chance of winning gold. Negative thoughts create negative actions. In competition, that can only result in a poor performance. So, if 60 000 people already believe you have no chance, surely it becomes impossible to remain positive?

Defending Olympic downhill champion Bernhard Russi of Switzerland was the third skier on the course and he went into an early lead with a time of 1:46:06. Another 11 skiers followed Russi, polishing the snow off the course as they went, unable to beat his time. Then it was Klammer. The crowd watched him crouch in the starting gate. He stared straight ahead, focusing on the icy course in front of him. The crowd held

their breath, collectively thinking, "It's too dangerous; he'll break his neck." What thoughts were in his head?

Klammer, known as 'The Klammer Express', shot out of the gate and threw himself down the mountain. His split time at 1000 metres was slower than Russi but he gamely carried on, seemingly fearless, and 60 000 gasps could be heard with every risk he took. But, as he neared the finish-line, the energy of the crowd was audibly changing once again and the deafening noise of 60 000 cheering spectators was sending an almighty surge of positive energy into the universe. He crossed the line in 1:45:73, beating Russi by .33 to take the gold medal.

> *"I thought I was going to crash all the way. I gave myself terrible frights"*
> **- Franz Klammer**

So he wasn't fearless after all. What then gave him the inner strength to give it his all: what allowed him to remain positive in a situation full of potential negatives? The answer lies in his understanding of the power of his mind. He *knew* he had the physical skill to win gold but crucially, he also had the mental skill to allow himself to do what he knew he was physically capable of doing. The energy of the crowd changed from positive to negative but from Klammer's point of view, nothing had actually changed. All of the potential negatives were out with his control; 15th skier to go - no point fretting about it, it just is; treacherously icy conditions - no point fretting about it, it just is. None of these things had actually changed who he was or changed his ability. He wasted no energy focusing on negative external factors, instead he concentrated totally on the internal factors he *could* control - his attitude. He maintained his own internal positive vibe: that's why he's an Olympic champion.

A POSITIVE INTERNAL VIBE IS THE 'INVISIBLE ARCHITECTURE OF SUCCESS'.

THE POWER OF *YOUR* MIND

Visualisation, also known as mental rehearsal, is a sports psychology technique that has been used to great effect for many years by top professionals in sport. Essentially, it's a learned mental skill that, when mastered, allows an athlete to 'see' their success as an action replay in their mind's-eye. However, applying this Law to the technique takes the concept of visualisation beyond simply 'seeing' success to actually experiencing it through the use of every sense - sight, smell, sound, touch, and perhaps even taste. It's widely accepted that to be most effective, visualisation sessions must focus on positive experiences that can be recounted through memory in the athlete's mind. This means that being able to re-live an actual winning moment by being able to re-create the processes that lead to that winning moment will be of much greater benefit than trying to visualise a set of circumstances that have yet to be realised. However, an inspired coach can help athletes to develop visualisation skills that allow every positive sight, sound, smell, touch, and taste experienced in training or in competition to be utilised and built into a 'winning' experience.

Young athletes or less experienced athletes may not have an actual winning experience to replay in their mind during a visualisation session so as their coach, it becomes important to encourage these athletes to focus on *every* positive experience they have. Just because they haven't yet won a javelin throwing competition doesn't mean they haven't experienced the *feel* of a winning javelin throw! A visualisation session can focus on any number of small positive moments that can be built into a bigger picture of success.

A bigger picture can be built on tiny details, for example:
- How did the javelin feel in your hand when you achieved a successful throw?
- What was in your line of vision as you prepared to throw?
- What could you hear on your run up?

It will often take a great number of throws to capture enough 'winning' moments to form a picture of success but focusing on being able to re-live each and every one of those moments through the use of visualisation can potentially bring even greater rewards than an actual winning experience. Research has shown that an athlete skilled in the use of visualisation techniques can continue to enhance the neural pathways that effectively train their body to perform a precise series of movements, without actually moving.

VISUALISE YOUR SUCCESS AND CREATE YOUR OWN INTERNAL POSITIVE VIBE.

Successful athletes don't just dream of success, they see it, hear it, smell, touch, and taste it too.

Champion golfer Jack Nicklaus has often said that he never takes a shot, in training or in competition, without first of all seeing that shot through his mind's eye and there are many other top players in a variety of sports who all agree that their winning performances are 'seen' many times before they become realities.

The vibrations created by thinking about an activity stimulate the brain to send electrical signals to the muscles involved in that activity, just as they would if the action was really taking place but without any actual movement occurring. This means that an added benefit of using visualisation is that the pattern of movements needed to create a successful action can be practiced without the muscles suffering physical fatigue in the process.

Competitive athletes use visualisation to prepare themselves for every eventuality at an event so that nothing on the day can throw a wet blanket over their internal positive vibe. They can prepare for noisy crowds, poor weather, and even for their performance not being up to scratch by creating a positive outcome for every situation. British javelin thrower Steve Backley is reported to have prepared by imagining himself to be in the last round of a major competition, in a losing position and with only one throw left. This could be viewed as a fairly negative situation but visualisation allowed him to 'see' his final throw being technically perfect and winning him the medal.

> *"Champions aren't made in gyms. Champions are made from something they have deep inside them - a desire, a dream, a vision"*
> **- Muhammad Ali, heavyweight boxing legend**

Ancient Way to Modern Day

In the 1960s, Dr Blaslotto conducted a visualisation study at the University of Chicago. He split a group of basketball players into three groups and then tested how many free-throws each group could make. The first group were then instructed to practice free-throws every day for one hour. The second group were instructed to visualise themselves taking free-throws every day. The third group were instructed to do nothing.

After 30 days, the groups were tested again. The first group had improved by 24 per cent, the second group by 23 per cent, and the third group showed no improvement.

Although this study has a number of flaws that make the evidence far from conclusive, what it does demonstrate is the remarkable power of the mind. The improvement in the second group was virtually the same as in the first group, yet the players in the second group had not physically practiced for 30 days.

Visualisation remains a key technique in modern sports psychology but the power of the mind has been at the heart of ancient words of wisdom throughout the ages. Over 100 years ago, James Allen wrote a book titled As A Man Thinketh, now regarded as the grandfather of all self-help books, and said;

Work joyfully and peacefully, knowing that right thoughts and right efforts will inevitably bring about right results.

Law Three

Top Performers Put Plans *Into Action*

Take Action

"The most important key to achieving great success is to decide upon your goal and launch, get started, take action, move"

- **John Wooden, basketball coach**

To achieve success in anything, you have to know what that success is going to look like when you achieve it. Otherwise, how will you know you've achieved it? You must create images in your mind of your dreams and your ambitions; your ultimate goals in life, and your vision of success must be a clear picture of what realising those dreams will bring into your life. However, turning a dream into a reality requires action, and that action must be inspired.

Look at it this way: if it's your goal to be a successful athlete, first of all you need to develop a clear picture of what being a successful athlete actually means to you. For example, does it mean winning an Olympic gold medal; holding a world record, or securing a lucrative contract as a professional? Next, you need to create a plan of action to get you from where you are now to where you want to be.

> **YOU HAVE TO KNOW WHERE YOU'RE GOING IN ORDER TO GET THERE - AND TO KNOW WHEN YOU'VE ARRIVED.**

The more inspired your goals are, the more passionate you are about achieving them. That passion generates the positive vibe and the positive energy that attracts positive things into your life. It's a Universal Law that when you focus your thoughts on positive things, you begin the process of bringing those things towards you and when you focus your actions on taking positive steps, you begin the process of moving forwards to meet the positive things that are already on their way to you. Clearly, without action, you're going nowhere, you're staying where you are. Not taking action equates to dreaming of winning a gold medal then taking up residence on your couch and waiting for it to materialise! Without action, your goals are destined to remain distant dreams but to bring them within your reach, the action you take must be focused action that takes you in the right direction. Action without focus equates to training for a marathon by following a 100 metre sprint training programme.

SPORTS SUCCESS = INTENTION + FOCUSED ACTION

Everyone has the potential to become great. As an athlete, you have the potential to become a great athlete but potential can become 'permanent' unless you take action to realise it. Athletes who display world class potential embark on training programmes designed to help them realise their full potential. A training programme can span several years so it's important that it's designed in such a way that motivation will be maintained throughout. Creating an action plan that incorporates stepping-stone goals to lead to-

wards the ultimate goal is an effective way of developing an athlete's skills, building their confidence, and keeping motivation high. Stepping-stone goals must be both challenging and achievable to inspire progress but *all* goals must represent another step towards achieving *your* dream.

Track athlete turned Ironman triathlete Dave Scott once said something along the lines of, "No one ever achieved anything by poking around aimlessly," in relation to fitness training. This is a statement that can be applied to all sports and to every level of participation. Whether your ultimate aim is to win an Olympic gold or to be able to run around your local park without stopping, the same need to set appropriate training targets along the way exists. Goal setting is a powerful method of maintaining motivation but it can only be truly effective if the goals set in place are inspirational to *you*. To avoid poking around aimlessly, you have to know what motivates you.

Successful people are motivated people and the most powerful form of motivation is self motivation. A coach can prepare a 'motivational' action plan for an athlete but unless the athlete feels inspired by the plan, it may not have the desired effect.

> **IT'S ALWAYS EASIER TO DO WHAT YOU WANT TO DO, RATHER THAN WHAT YOU HAVE TO DO.**

When you find your source of inspiration, you will also find your source of motivation. You are inspired by the things you feel most passionate about and you will find you are motivated to take action on the things you feel most passionate about. Successful people are passionate about what they do: successful people love what they do and they do what they love. Find what you love and you will find what motivates you.

TYPES OF MOTIVATION

So what *really* motivates you as a sportsperson? You can probably give lots of reasons for being involved in sport but you might need to delve a little deeper to discover what the *real* reasons are.

Are you an in-y or an out-y?
Motivation is sometimes described as being intrinsic or extrinsic.
Intrinsic motivation:
Intrinsic motivation comes from within, so you could say from the inside out. If you're intrinsically motivated, you're someone who's involved in sport for the love of it. Taking part gives you a "buzz" and it's the sheer enjoyment, thrill, or even challenge of your sport that motivates you to stay involved. As a competitor, you may feel "driven" to perform and "hungry" for success. It's all about your emotions. You *love* your sport.

Extrinsic motivation:

Extrinsic motivation comes from external sources, so you could say from the outside in. If you're extrinsically motivated, you're someone who's involved in sport for what it can bring you *beyond* simple enjoyment. You're motivated by prize money, trophies, awards and recognition. As a competitor, a lack of big prize money might also create a lack of motivation. It's all about external rewards. You *love* the trappings of your sport.

Ask yourself a couple of questions -
1. If your skill level was such that you were unlikely to ever make the Olympic squad, would you stay involved in your sport?
2. The results of your qualifying rounds in a competition now mean you have no chance of achieving the top prize, would you continue to give your 'all' in the remaining rounds?

If you answered 'yes' to both of the above questions then your motivation is intrinsic. But, did you answer 'yes' to the second question because you're secretly hoping there might be a talent scout in the crowd? If so, the source of your motivation becomes extrinsic.

Of course, it's quite possible to be an in-y *and* an out-y. Understanding what motivates you is rarely as simple as being either one or the other. Neither intrinsic nor extrinsic motivation can explain what keeps an ultra-distance runner going when they're close to exhaustion, their feet are bleeding, and the race winner already crossed the finish-line 24 hours ago. Clearly, big prize money is no longer motivating them to continue and it's unlikely they're actually experiencing much enjoyment by that stage, so what drives them? To find an answer, further delving is required.

Are you in it to win it?
Another way to look at motivation is to consider whether it comes from

primary or secondary sources.

Primary motivation:

Whatever your sport, primary motivation is derived from the activity itself. It's the challenge of the sport that motivates rather than the need to win or beat others. It's primary motivation that keeps golfers of all ages and abilities out on the course for hours every weekend. The satisfaction of perfecting a swing or playing a great shot is enough to maintain motivation without the need to be in direct competition with anyone else.

Secondary motivation:

Secondary motivation comes from everything that may be influencing your involvement in sport other than the activity itself. Sources can be your coach, your peers, team-mates, the audience, trophies, medals, and prize money.

The ultra-distance runner with the bleeding feet is motivated to continue by primary sources. The challenge of the event provides the motivation to keep going, even when conditions are pretty grim and winning is no longer an option. The same can be said of the Ironman triathlete, the solo yachtsman, or the mountain climber. For the golfer, however, the source of motivation might not be so clear. The motivation to spend hours out on the course honing skills could be derived simply from the satisfaction of mastering the game (primary) but it could also be coming from a desire to win a big tournament (secondary).

As you can see, motivation is a complex subject. There isn't always going to be a cut and dry answer to the question of what motivates you as a sportsperson, but it's a question that's worth deliberating over none-the-less. In terms of becoming a winner in sport, knowing what *really* motivates you will give you a clearer indication of your level of commitment to your sport.

UNDERSTAND YOUR PASSION TO UNDERSTAND YOUR INSPIRATION AND YOUR MOTIVATION.

Are you a sticker or a quitter?

Both primary and secondary sources of motivation can be either positive or negative and this in itself can have a big influence on your ability to *stay* motivated.

Positive primary motivation

If you're motivated by the satisfaction of performing well in your sport, then a good performance is all it takes to keep your motivation high.

Negative primary motivation

Now imagine you haven't been performing too well for a while, what happens to your motivation? If you are motivated by the satisfaction of improving your skills or perfecting your technique, a long spell of not achieving that level of performance or of not experiencing the "buzz" will have a negative effect. In fact, if you're no longer feeling satisfied by your performance, will you stick with the sport?

Positive secondary motivation

A noisy, supportive crowd is a great example of positive secondary motivation. Knowing a huge number of spectators are there rooting for you can have a powerfully motivating effect. If your coach is supporting you, or your team-mates are behind you, motivation is much easier to maintain.

Negative secondary motivation

On the flip side, a noisy non-supportive crowd can be just as powerfully de-motivating. How else can you explain the advantages of playing in front of a home crowd in sports such as football, or the disadvantages of playing away matches? By the same token, if you feel your coach isn't supporting your decisions or your team-mates aren't behind you as a player, you may struggle to remain motivated.

The journey to the top of your game is not guaranteed to be a straight or a smooth one. Motivation is naturally going to be boosted by your successes along the way but your ability to stay motivated through the tough times and the inevitable lows depends largely on how you choose to deal with setbacks - in other words, your attitude. This is covered in more detail later in **Law Eleven**.

> *"Ability is what you're capable of doing. Motivation determines what you do. Attitude determines how you will do it"*
> **- Lou Holte, American football coach**

Successful sportspeople often use the words 'driven' and 'compelled' to describe their involvement in sport. Their love of their sport and their passion for what they do is what 'drives' them to take action and to achieve their dreams. Their motivation to succeed and their will to win is such that on occasion, sports fans and spectators witness truly inspirational performances that have a motivational effect on many others and for a long time after the event.

Tour de Force

In 2005, Lance Armstrong won the Tour de France cycle race for the seventh consecutive time. He'd already broken all previous records with his sixth win the previous year so his seventh victory was an outstanding sporting achievement. Maintaining the motivation to train and compete at top level in such a gruelling event is remarkable in itself but even more so when you realise that in 1996 he was diagnosed with testicular cancer and given only a 40 per cent chance of survival. Only two years later in 1998, he was back on his bike and in serious training for racing. The rest, as they say, is history.

"Pain is temporary, quitting lasts forever" - **Lance Armstrong**

Down But Not Out

In the 1992 Barcelona Olympics, British athlete Derek Redmond was a real medal contender in the 400 metres event. He'd been through eight operations for a variety of injuries over a four year period but he felt he was in the shape of his life. He ran the fastest time in the first round and won his quarter-final, so hopes were high as he lined up to compete in the semi-final. He started the race well but in the final 250 metres, his hamstring snapped. In obvious pain, he hobbled to a halt and fell to the ground. Stretcher-bearers made their way to him on the track but he astonished spectators by getting to his feet and making a determined effort to finish the race. He was joined on the track by his father, who had barged passed all security measures, and together they made their way around the track to receive a standing ovation from 65 000 cheering spectators as they crossed the finish-line. Although the record books state he 'did not finish' due to having been assisted by his father, the viewing public know differently. Derek Redmond finished his race.

"Everything I had worked for was finished. I hated everybody. I hated the world. I hated hamstrings. I hated it all. I felt so bitter that I was injured again. I told myself I had to finish. I kept hopping round. Then, with 100 metres to go, I felt a hand on my shoulder. It was my old man" - **Derek Redmond**

Ancient Way to Modern Day

In 1995, the Sport Motivation Scale (SMS) was developed to assess an athlete's level of intrinsic motivation. The results can help a coach to understand how an athlete's level of motivation may be affecting their performance. The SMS was revised in 2007 and remains a popular tool to help measure motivation in sport.

The greatest motivation has always been self-motivation and it's a sentiment that echoes through history in a great many wise old sayings. An ancient Burmese saying is;

Who aims at excellence will be above mediocrity; who aims at mediocrity will be far short of it.

Law Four

As You Think, You Become

Think Like A Winner

"Before you can win a game, you have to not lose it"

- Chuck Noll, American football player and coach

It's a Universal Law that our outer world is a reflection of our inner world. This means if your outer world is one of chaos and calamity, it's a direct reflection of the chaos and calamity that's going on in your inner world - your mind.

In sport, if you have low self-esteem or feel badly about yourself in any way or find that your daily life is filled with anger, loathing or hatred, then your outer world is a place of matching turmoil. It becomes self-perpetuating: you feel bad so your outer world becomes bad so you feel worse…! The happenings of your inner world - your mind - correspond directly with the happenings of your outer world - your reality.

YOU ARE AS YOU THINK YOU ARE AND YOUR CIRCUMSTANCES ARE AS YOU THINK THEY ARE.

Picture the scene: you're an athlete and you're on target to achieving your goal of being selected for the Olympic training squad. Training has been going well and you've been producing consistently good results. You've achieved a personal best performance this season *and*, crucially, you've remained injury free. The recurring injury that prevented you from making the team last time around appears finally to be behind you. You're feeling in the form of your life.

Then you have a bad training day. In fact, your bad day begins before you even get to your training session. You wake up that morning feeling more tired than when you went to bed after a restless night of bad dreams revolving around not making the  team. Even though you know it was just a dream, you're unable to shake the enormously heavy feeling of bitter disappointment you experienced. You then get held up, through no fault of your own, on your way to the training ground and arrive late. Your coach lets you, and everyone within earshot, know just how disappointing your late arrival is and questions your commitment to the selection process. Your mood is now at an all time low and you proceed to put in some of your all-time worst performances ever in training. You feel in the worst form of your life and, just to add injury to insult, that old injury begins to niggle.

So what happened? In the space of a few hours you've gone from feeling in top form and on track to achieving your Olympic dream to feeling you're at the bottom of a pit of despair and a million miles from realising your dream. Is it physically possible to lose all condition in such a short period of time? Of course not, but it *is* mentally possible. Your emotional state has had a dramatic effect on your physical state. You've effectively gone through your day physically and mentally *living* your dream - you've been dwelling on the disappointment and re-living it over and over again in your mind. The weight of that disappointment has not only exhausted you mentally, it has also affected your whole demeanour and your physical ability to function normally, let alone to the best of your ability.

Your 'poor' emotional state led to your 'poor' physical performance. Because of your low mood, the wrath of your coach served as confirmation that you've been right to dwell on thoughts of disappointment all day. You're feeling disappointed, your coach is disappointed, therefore your 'logical' conclusion is that you are indeed a disappointment. Your thoughts are totally irrational and doubly so because you boarded that train of thought in a dream - nothing is based on reality! Your inner world is now reflected in your outer world: your reality is a reflection of your thinking. This serves to highlight the extraordinary power of the mind.

Think of it this way; if you had dreamed of winning Olympic gold, how would that have affected your mood? If you had gone through your day feeling positively inspired by your dream, how would your coach's comments have affected you? Chances are you'd have been riled by having your commitment questioned, especially when the circumstances that delayed you were out with your control, but you'd have felt even *more* motivated to demonstrate your commitment and your readiness for selection.

Your physical state is unquestionably governed by your emotional state, but what about that niggling injury? The real question is; did the niggle physically reappear in isolation or did it come as part of a 'disappointment package'? If you've suffered the disappointment of failing to make squad selection before because of a recurring injury problem, the train of thought you boarded in your dream will take you right back to that point in your life and recreate everything you felt at that time, both emotionally *and* physically.

Clearly, positive thoughts are the driving force behind positive performances but in the high pressure environment of competitive sport, it's not *always* going to be possible to prevent negative thoughts from entering your mind. The key is to accept each thought for what it is, a thought. A thought can enter your mind but a thought can also *leave* your mind. Thoughts might hang around in your mind for a while but with practice, you can learn to identify the good, the bad, and the ugly and learn to evict the unhelpful variety *before* they start to get comfortable in there.

Ever heard the expression, 'Hell on a handcart'? It's used to describe a situation that's going from bad to worse, and out of control. Well, think about that for a moment. If your train of thought has got you on a handcart to somewhere you don't want to go, who's controlling your handcart? The clue is in your mode of transport - it's a handcart. **Stop powering it.**

The more time you spend dwelling on a thought, the more power you're giving it. You might not be able to halt it instantly but the moment you stop powering it, you begin to slow down. You can't always control the thoughts that enter your head but you can control where those thoughts take you. If you're not enjoying the ride, you *can* choose to get off at the next station.

> **BY CHANGING YOUR THINKING, YOU CAN CHANGE YOUR REALITY.**

By taking control of your mind, you can take control of all aspects of your life. Negative thinking corresponds with a negative reality, therefore, positive thinking corresponds with a positive reality. Whatever you choose to focus on, you give energy to. The more energy you give a thought, the more life you give it and the more 'real' it begins to feel. Shift your focus: focus on what you want in life, not what you don't want. Focus on what you have, not what you don't have. Focus on what you can do, not what you can't do.

> *"Do not let what you cannot do interfere with what you can do"*
> **- John Wooden, basketball coach**

THE SUCCESS CYCLE

Research into the psychology of sport has shown that an athlete's potential performance can be traced through something known as the success cycle. The cycle basically highlights the relationship between how an athlete feels about themselves and how they are likely to perform. So, in sport psychology terms, the cycle would revolve around the following:

...positive self-image →
positive attitude →

> **positive expectations** →
> **improved behaviour** →
> **enhanced performance...**

In real terms, for an athlete in training, this translates into:

> **...feeling good about yourself** →
> **feeling confident about your ability** →
> **believing you can produce an improved performance** →
> **focusing on giving yourself every opportunity by eating well;**
> **sleeping well; remaining motivated through training** →
> **producing a personal best...**

Now take a moment to consider the corresponding effects of beginning the cycle with a negative self-image. The power of the mind remains! By changing the quality of your thoughts, you can change the quality of your life.

To fully understand the principle behind 'As You Think, You Become', it's important to understand the significance of the word 'you'. Only *you* can control *your* inner world so only *you* can control *your* outer world. You must take responsibility for your circumstances and not look for other people or other things to blame for anything that's not the way you want it to be. You're the only one who can control your thoughts so you're the only one responsible for your circumstances. To change *your* reality, you must change *your* thoughts.

How anyone interprets success and failure is very much a personal choice but studies have shown that in sport, winners tend to attribute their success to their own actions whereas losers have a greater tendency to attribute their lack of success to the actions of others as well as themselves. For example, a winner might say, "I won because I played well," but a loser might say, "I lost because I played badly... and the ref' was blind!"

The attributions given by an athlete can also help a coach better understand the athlete's emotions. Has the result affected motivation? Is this result likely to have an effect on future performance? One of the cornerstones of good coaching is the development of confidence and the all important positive self-image in athletes, so how the coach analyses a below expectation result needs careful consideration. Allowing an athlete the opportunity to analyse their own performance and voice their own thoughts on a poorer than expected result will be of far greater benefit than wading in with, "You played like an idiot and deserved to lose!"

Attributions can be described as either stable or unstable. Below are two examples of attributions a player may give after a winning result:

"I was a bit lucky to win that last game."
This would be described as an unstable attribution as the use of the word 'luck' suggests little confidence in being able to produce the same winning result in a future performance.
"That game has confirmed my technique is sound."
This would be described as a stable attribution as the confirmation of the player's ability suggests greater confidence in producing a future winning performance.

The same logic can be applied to attributions given after a losing result. If failure is attributed to poor technique or low skill it clearly suggests the athlete feels failure will be the most likely result in future performances - confidence has been knocked. Their inner 'low' will be reflected in their outer reality.

When unstable, negative attributions are being voiced by an athlete, it becomes the job of the coach to help turn them into more stable, positive versions. An athlete's lack of confidence can quickly lead to a lack of motivation and could even cause some individuals to give up on their sport completely. Goal setting can be helpful but, as you know from the **Law Three**, goals can only be truly effective if they are goals that inspire the athlete. Ultimately, if you are that athlete, only you can change *your* reality and changing your reality means changing *your* thinking.

To begin making changes, try the following -

- take a hard, objective look at your current reality then ask yourself, 'how are my inner thoughts and attitudes being reflected in my outer life?'
- take responsibility for your reality and commit to making changes in that reality by choosing to change your thinking
- begin to visualise the world you want; focus your mind on the positive things you want in order to bring those positive things into your reality
- ask yourself, ' what changes will I need to make internally to achieve the changes I want externally?'
- take steps to make those changes: take action!

By thinking and talking only about what you want and refusing to think or talk about what you don't want, you become the architect of your own destiny.

"THE MINUTE YOU START THINKING ABOUT WHAT YOU'LL DO IF YOU LOSE, YOU'VE LOST"

Champion track cyclist Sir Chris Hoy is a great example of an athlete who takes total responsibility for his reality by taking control of his thinking. He's renowned for his meticulous race preparation, both physically and mentally, and he knows it sets him apart from his opponents. However, he also knows he's being studied. He's the one to beat so he knows his opponents are looking for ways to beat him. His strength remains his ability to

remain focused only on what he can control; his focus is on riding and controlling his own race. Hoy's calm, controlled outer world is a reflection of his calm, controlled inner world. In effect, by the time Hoy lines up on the race start-line, his preparation is so complete, he's already won.

After winning his 10th track cycling gold medal at the World Championships in Copenhagen, the very place he won his first cycling gold, he was asked in an interview how it felt to achieve such a landmark victory:

"I'm delighted. I was aware of the magnitude of a 10th world title... because it's been in the press and people have been asking me about it... but it was only when someone asked me 'what does it feel like to have 10' when I'd finished that it registered because I was so focused on the race itself. That's the key really, to be focused on the process and not worrying about the outcome"

His 10th gold medal was perhaps his hardest earned yet. His event, the Keirin, is not for the feint-hearted and competitors expect a bit of rough and tumble as they jostle for position on the track. However, Hoy was dumped on his backside during qualifying rounds by an opponent trying to prevent him from reaching his favourite position as the race started.

"That was out of order," **said Hoy.** *"It did make me angry, but that's another emotion you try and keep in check - you don't want to let the red mist descend and lose the plot, you've got to stay controlled and focused"*

Learning how to stay controlled and focused - in every imaginable circumstance - is all part of Hoy's race preparation plan and it's also a huge contributing factor to his sporting success.

> *"The episode did frustrate the usually placid, gentlemanly Hoy, but - after years under the tutelage of Dr Steve Peters, the British Cycling psychiatrist - he controlled his inner chimp"*
> **- Brendan Gallagher, The Telegraph**

His opponent's ploy to rob him of his favourite racing position was just one of many deliberate attempts made to unsettle Hoy in all of his Copenhagen races. He's the man of the moment, the one to beat, so all eyes are on him. Many of his opponent's will be studying video recordings of him in action as part of their own race preparation. They'll study how he rides, research his race tactics, and plan their own races around trying to 'block' Hoy. Of course, if they really want to get over the finish-line ahead of him; if they want a gold medal to be *their* reality, they will need to study what it takes to *think* like Hoy.

POSITIVE MENTAL ATTITUDE

We've already established that positive thoughts lead to positive actions and that positive actions lead to positive outcomes but learning how to see things positively doesn't mean wearing rose-tinted glasses. In fact, it means being able to see things exactly as they are. With a positive mental attitude, you are able to see the potential to change your reality. With a positive mental attitude, you are able to see the correlation between your outer world and your inner world and you are open to making the internal changes needed to bring you the external changes you want.

THINKING POSITIVELY ALLOWS POSITIVE CHANGES TO BE MADE.

When you are able to think positively, even analysing a less than perfect result remains a positive, motivational experience. With a positive mental attitude, you focus on your strengths and you are able to see any areas of weakness you identify as opportunities to learn and improve. With a negative mental attitude, analysing a disappointing result becomes a negative, de-motivating experience with all of your focus on your failures. If your inner world is in turmoil, your outer world can only reflect that turmoil.

THINK HAPPY, BE HAPPY!

In the 1994 Lillehammer winter Olympics, the Japanese 120 metre ski jump team had a convincing lead in the final event with only one jump remaining. That jump belonged to Masahiko Harada, affectionately known as 'Happy Harada' due to his infectious grin. In his previous jump, Harada had cleared 122 metres and needed a jump of only 110 metres to secure the gold medal for Japan. He cleared 97.5 metres - the worst jump of the entire event - and Germany won gold.

> *"In the past, a well-raised Japanese would have to commit hari-kari after such a mistake. Today nobody expects that of us"*
> **- Masahiko Harada**

So what happened? Did the wind change at a crucial moment; was it just a bad jump, or did the pressure get to him?

Many top class athletes with proven ability and countless winning performances behind them have choked when it really mattered - at the Olympics. Perhaps it's the sheer scale of the event that creates unbearable pressure; the weight of expectation; the knowledge that an entire nation of supporters are counting on them to bring home a medal. Whatever the catalyst, choking describes the moment that self-doubt kicks in. Negative thoughts creep into your head and take over. The voice in your head says, "You can't do this, you're not ready" - and you believe it. Everything positive that should be brought to the forefront of your mind vanishes into thin air. The fact that you *are* ready and you *can* do it gets railroaded into oblivion by the power of negative thinking and the negative thoughts manifest themselves into negative actions, resulting in a poor performance. Your negative thinking becomes your negative reality.

Four years later, Harada was back on the Olympic stage in the 1998 winter games in Nagano. Since his disappointing performance in 1994, he'd gone on to win numerous world cup events and a world championship so there was no doubt he was a class act. The Japanese team were already in the lead as Harada prepared to take his first jump. He managed a pitiful 79.5 metres and the team dropped from first to fifth place. Was it just a cruel coincidence? Did the wind turn against him at the wrong moment yet again? Or did he just buckle under pressure?

Now take a moment to consider how Harada must have felt as he prepared to take his second jump. Was history about to repeat itself? The team's chances of winning a medal depended on his next jump - could he do it?

He sped down the ramp and landed a massive 137 metre jump putting the team into a virtually unbeatable lead. Team mate Kazuyoshi Funaki took the final jump and cleared 125 metres to secure the gold medal for the Japanese team. What was it that allowed Funaki to hold his nerve when the pressure was on? What was it that prevented Harada from choking once more under increasing pressure? The answers lie in understanding and applying this Law and adopting a positive mental attitude.

Ancient Way to Modern Day

A recent study undertaken by researchers at Bishop's University in Canada, and published in Athletic Insight, looked at the relationship between self-esteem and exercise activity. Their findings were that there was a positive relationship between exercise activity and self-esteem and that a higher level of exercise activity is associated with a higher level of self-esteem.

The effects of self-image on sports performance continue to be studied and the results continue to support the theory that how an athlete 'sees' themselves has the potential to impact their performance in competition. What an athlete believes becomes their reality and this is a message that appears in the teachings of a great many ancient philosophers.

In more recent history, inspirational spiritual leader Mahatma Gandhi expressed the same principle when he said;

A man is but the product of his thoughts.
What he thinks, he becomes.

Law Five

You Get Out What You Put In

Give It Your Best Effort

"You find that you have peace of mind and can enjoy yourself, get more sleep, rest when you know that it was a one hundred percent effort that you gave - win or lose"

- Gordie Howe, ice hockey player

Nobody gets to the top of their game without effort. Olympic athletes don't get to step up onto the medal podium without years of dedicated training and professional sportspeople don't get to sign lucrative long-term contracts without first earning their keep. Becoming a champion athlete is not something that 'just happens' and there's no such thing as an overnight success. Getting to the top is a process and it's a process governed by the principle that you get out of life what you put in to life.

It's a Universal Law that *nothing* happens by chance. In all areas of life, there's a reason for everything that happens and in effect, you reap what you sow. In sport, this means that winners don't just win by chance and losers don't just lose by chance; there are *reasons* for a winning or a losing result. Winners become winners because of what they routinely do. They become winners because of their habitual positive thought processes and positive actions: they become winners because they work hard at practicing and developing 'winning ways' in everything they do.

IF YOU FAIL TO PREPARE, YOU PREPARE TO FAIL.

There's a common expression, 'fail to prepare, prepare to fail', so it's a well known fact that preparation is the key to success. A Texan oil billionaire once said;

"There are three secrets to success. First, individuals have to decide exactly what it is they want from a certain situation - not roughly or vaguely, but specifically. Then they have to work out what costs or sacrifices would be needed to get these things. Finally, they have to be prepared to pay those costs and make those sacrifices."

I think it's fair to say that most athletes are prepared to take steps one and two but perhaps the difference between success and failure comes down to how willing each individual is to take step three.

Effective preparation in competitive sport is all about establishing effective success habits. Considerable research has been done in this area and results show that keeping a daily training diary can be enormously helpful. A diary allows goals to be set on a daily basis and makes recording results a form of daily analysis. The goals can be related to any area of life - work, home, personal - as well as sport or training but ultimately they should serve the purpose of maintaining commitment to the 'big goal' being prepared for. This sort of daily focus helps to keep *everything* on track and makes sure that every day counts as a day of preparation. In the words of soccer superstar Pele, "Everything is practice for the game." Becoming a winner takes more than winning a race, you must be a winner every day and in every way.

In most sports, far more time will be spent in training than will ever be spent in actual competition so getting the most out of each training session is of vital importance if a drift into just going through the motions is to be avoided. This can also be termed 'intelligent effort', meaning that knowing exactly what action to take allows you to leverage your energy in training to generate the greatest impact on your performance. It's a concept known as the Pareto principle or the '80-20 rule' and it was proposed by Joseph Juran, a business management thinker, who developed an observation made in 1906 by an Italian economist, named Pareto, that 80 per cent of the land in Italy was owned by 20 per cent of the population. Juran discovered that 20 per cent of the pea-pods in his garden produced 80 per cent of the peas! The 80-20 rule is now a common rule-of-thumb in business with 80 per cent of a company's sales acknowledged to come from 20 per cent of the company's clients and it's a principle that can be applied equally well to sports training. With intelligent effort, 20 per cent of your training efforts will yield an 80 per cent improvement in your performance. At least one goal should be set for each session and preparation for that session must include getting the athlete's 'head into gear' so they can focus on the session's key elements. Keeping the focus on goals specific to each individual session makes it easier for an athlete to gauge their progress. This regular, positive experience can also help to improve self-image which will, in turn, begin a positive success cycle.

Some athletes prefer to simply set themselves a target for each training session as they begin their warm-up but whatever method is used, the idea is to provide focus and then maintain that focus throughout every stage of training and preparation. Preparation for competition begins a *long* time before the date of the big event itself so as the Texan oil billionaire pointed out, success can only come to those who are prepared to make a long-term commitment. Basketball coach Pat Riley once said, *"There are only two options regarding commitment. You're either IN or you're OUT, there's no such thing as life IN-BETWEEN,"* but Big Wave surfer Laird Hamilton perhaps said it best…

…YOU ARE EITHER ON THE WAVE OR OFF THE WAVE, YOU CAN'T BE KINDA ON IT.

How committed you are to your sport and to becoming the best you can be will also be reflected in how you interpret success and failure. In the last chapter, the importance of maintaining a positive mental attitude under all circumstances was highlighted but ultimately, developing your ability to think positively comes down to developing an understanding of your mindset.

Research into the definitions of sporting success has concluded that athletes tend to strive for three main goals:

Mastery

Mastery or task goals are those associated with self-improvement so success can be measured by a good performance - irrespective of whether it's a winning one or not. Athletes with a mastery-oriented goal strive to *improve* their ability or performance.

Ego

Ego or ability goals are associated with demonstrating high ability and performing better than rivals - winning! Athletes with an ego-oriented goal strive to *prove* their ability.

Social approval

A social approval goal is that of an athlete who strives to please others with their performance. This could be a coach or parents and young children in sport are thought to be strongly motivated in this way.

Many athletes find themselves motivated by both mastery and ego-oriented goals. A good example is Linford Christie when he won silver in the 1988 Olympics. In an interview afterwards he said he'd certainly run to win, and obviously believed he could win, which suggests an ego-oriented goal. However, his delight at having beaten his own personal best and becoming the first European to run 100 metres in under ten seconds clearly demonstrates a mastery-oriented goal.

Carol Dweck is a world-renowned psychologist and in her book, 'Mindset: The New Psychology Of Success', she tells of her findings after decades of research into achievement and success, and the discovery of how an individual's mindset holds the key to realising both.

Mindset can be split into two categories:

Fixed Mindset

A person in a fixed mindset believes that they're stuck with their lot.

Any mediocre skills, talent or ability they may have are just what they were born with and nothing will change that. The same can be said of an extremely skilled, talented or able individual with a fixed mindset. They too believe their abilities are just a given and not something they need to work at.

> *"Think about your intelligence, talents, and personality.*
> *Are they just fixed or can you develop them?"*
> **- Carol Dweck**

Growth Mindset

A person with a growth mindset believes that who they are and where they are now can potentially be changed with dedication and effort. Even if they are already particularly talented in some way, they still believe that further learning and practice can lead to greater things.

In the early stages of her research into 'Mindset', Carol Dweck gave a classroom of children a challenging task to complete. When the mastery-oriented goal was emphasised, so self-improvement, the children displayed high effort and great perseverance to complete the task. When a similar task was given but an ego-oriented goal emphasised, the reaction to the challenge became entirely dependent on the children's own perceptions of how good they were - known as perceived ability. Children with high perceived ability did well but rejected the opportunity to improve their skills if it meant they might make a mistake in public. Children with low perceived ability did badly and tended to give up completely.

This early experiment, equally relevant to a sports environment, demonstrated that mastery-oriented goals were preferable to ego-oriented goals in terms of maintaining motivation. Further research confirmed Dweck's discovery that individuals have either a fixed or a growth mindset and that without a growth mindset, further learning and improvement of skills is unlikely. Clearly, a fixed mindset is not conducive to developing an athlete's true potential. To realise a top performance, athletes must be encouraged to understand and embrace the benefits of a growth mindset.

Picture the scene: you're a talented young athlete, you've already won your school championship, your club championship, and your county championship. You've become a big fish in a small pond so it's time to compete nationally
- *how are you feeling?*

Chances are you feel pretty confident. After all, you've got a proven track record, a tried and tested winning formula. You enter a national event and cross the finishing line in the middle third of the pack
- *now how are you feeling?*

The answer to the last question depends entirely on your mindset. Clearly, you've become a small fish in a big pond. Your current mindset will determine how that makes you feel.

If you have a fixed mindset, you'll judge yourself harshly after the disappointing race result. Your best wasn't good enough so maybe you should just give up?

If you have a growth mindset, you'll view the disappointing race result as an opportunity to learn; an opportunity to make changes and to improve. Your *current* best wasn't good enough so it's time to up your game.

Your mindset can hold you back. It can mean the difference between staying where you are now or moving on to realise your full potential. Making the move from being a middle of the pack finisher to a frontrunner is a three step process.

Step One - Take Action

If you want things to change, you have to make changes. If you carry on doing things the same way, things will stay the same. Take action. You can analyse your performance until the cows come home but nothing is going to change until you *do* something.

Step Two - Learn From The Best

Make a study of successful sportspeople using neuro-linguistic programming methodologies and NLP sports models of excellence. What is it that makes race winners, winners?

Step Three - Adapt

Armed with a clear action plan and an understanding of what it takes to get to the front of the pack, it's time to adapt. Apply what you know to your training and make the necessary changes.

> " *I found out that if you are going to win games,*
> *you had better be ready to adapt*"
> **- Scotty Bowman, ice hockey coach**

How willing you are to make changes equates to how committed you are to your sport and how willing you are to do whatever it takes to succeed: it indicates how much you're prepared to put in.

> **If you want more, put more in…**
> **…be prepared to make changes in order**
> **to get what you want.**
>
> *Herschel Walker is a former NFL running back and a Collegiate Football Hall of Fame player. When he was in junior high school, he already knew he wanted to play football but the coach told him he was too small*

and advised him to try out for track instead. But, instead of giving up, Herschel dedicated himself to an intensive training programme - reported to include push ups, sit ups, and sprint running - in a committed effort to build himself up. Only a few years later, he won the Heisman trophy, the most prestigious award in college football awarded annually to the most outstanding player in the US.

Ancient Way to Modern Day

The science behind this Law is known by the term 'cause and effect'. It's a term used to describe the philosophical concept of causality which, in a nutshell, states that for every action there is an equal and opposite effect. If you hit your hand with a hammer (cause), your hand hurts (effect)!

It's also a spiritual concept at the heart of Buddhism with the law of karmic cause and effect which essentially teaches that you're responsible for your own life and the circumstances you are in. The basic idea is that positive causes lead to positive effects and negative causes lead to negative effects and that only you are responsible for the creation of those causes, whether positive or negative - exactly as in modern sports psychology.

A huge number of ancient sayings and proverbs revolve around this principle, not least, 'You reap what you sow', but you may also be familiar with, 'What goes around, comes around'. The Dalai Lama once said;

Happiness is not something ready made.
It comes from your own actions.

Law Six

Winning Efforts Receive Winning Rewards

Earn Your Reward

"Gold medals aren't really made of gold. They're made of sweat, determination, and a hard-to-find alloy called guts"
- Dan Gable, amateur wrestler

Just as it's a Universal Law that you get out what you put in, it 's also a Law that you will be compensated for what you put in. The principle of this Law is that you will always be rewarded commensurately with your efforts so in sport, this means that high quality effort will be rewarded with high quality results but low quality effort will only ever achieve low quality results.

Some good examples of this Law in action can be found in a study of regular "gym rats." If you visit your local gym on any given day, you will find at least one member who appears to have become part of the furniture. They're the ones who seem to be there every day and seem to be there for hours every time - yet they never seem  to progress in terms of improving their fitness or of changing their body shape. They struggle to understand why one of their gym acquaintances has made enormous progress with their training plan yet they only go to the gym three times a week and spend no more than one hour there each time; surely going more often should be getting bigger and better results than going less often?

IT'S NOT THE HOURS YOU PUT IN, IT'S WHAT YOU PUT INTO THE HOURS.

This all too common scenario illustrates this Law perfectly and demonstrates that a winning effort has little to do with quantity of effort but everything to do with quality of effort. Let's call our gym rat Bob. Bob has always considered himself to be a bit on the scrawny side and joined the gym in an effort to build a bit of muscle to bulk his body up a bit. He wants to be more muscular because he lacks confidence in himself and he feels he suffered at the hands of bullies in his schooldays because of his size. So, Bob knows he wants to bulk up but does he know what his goal is *specifically*? He knows that he doesn't want to be bullied and that he doesn't have much self-confidence but does he know what he *wants*: does he know what a confident version of himself looks like?

YOU HAVE TO KNOW EXACTLY WHAT YOU WANT - NOT ROUGHLY OR VAGUELY, BUT SPECIFICALLY.

It takes an inspired vision of success to be able to take inspired action to achieve that success. To succeed, Bob needs a clear vision of what that success looks like. To be able to take effective action, he needs to know exactly what it is he's aiming to achieve. Currently, Bob holds a negative image of being bullied at school in his mind. He's creating a negative vibe in everything he does; he's generating negative energy through his thoughts by focusing on what he doesn't want. His lack of positive results is the outcome. To be able to realise his dream, Bob has to know what that dream is. Dreaming of not being bullied at school is completely useless in terms of inspiring success because he's now 30 years old and those days are gone, they can't be changed. To be able to make the changes to his body shape that he wants, Bob needs a positive vision of what making those changes will bring him now. He needs a clear mental image of what his success looks like, feels like, sounds like, smells and tastes like. It's only after he learns to think positively that he can then take positive action to turn his dream into a reality.

Bob has to know where he's going to be able to get there and he has to know what it is he wants, exactly, to be able to create an effective plan of action that will get him, step-by-step, from where he is now to where he wants to be. He believes he's giving it his all by going to the gym for endless hours every day but what is he actually *giving*; what is he actually *doing* while he's in the gym? Without a vision and without positive focus, he's 'poking around aimlessly' and receiving very little return for his efforts. By simply upping the quality of his efforts, he would up the quality of his return. In Bob's case, less really could be more.

The same principle still applies even when a clear vision of success *has* been formed. Once you know what you want and you know what you have to do to achieve it, you have to commit to *doing* it. For example, if someone joins a gym with the goal of losing weight and they have a clear vision of what their success will look like, they are well on their way to achieving that success. They follow their exercise regime faithfully and put a total positive effort into each session but they're not receiving the expected results in terms of weight loss. They're putting in a quality effort but not receiving a quality return, why not? The answer lies in their *total* commitment to achieving their goal. Clearly they're committed to following an exercise programme but what about the other elements of their weight loss action plan? Are they committed to following a healthy eating plan? Are they thinking positively about what substituting their favourite foods with healthier alternatives will bring them or are they focusing on what they can't have; what they're 'missing out' on? Of course, it could also be that they feel so good about themselves after each exercise session that they celebrate their achievement each time with a cream cake - or two! In this case, total commitment to one aspect of their action plan but not *all* aspects does not constitute a quality effort so quality results cannot be received in return.

IT TAKES TOTAL DEDICATION TO ACHIEVE TOTAL PAYBACK.

HOLDING BACK

So what about a committed, dedicated athlete who gives their all in training and receives quality results in return for their quality efforts but then fails to achieve the expected results in competition? In fact, they under-achieve, and when this is the case, it suggests that the quality of effort given when under competitive pressure is not the same as the quality of effort given in practice. What causes an athlete to 'hold back' when it matters most?

The answer lies in the athlete's brain and in one area of the brain in particular, an area referred to as the lizard brain. This is a term used to describe the part of your brain concerned with basic survival. Your lizard brain doesn't want you to take any chances in life or do anything risky, it wants you to play it safe and just stay alive - no matter how dull that life may be - and it's the voice in the back of your head telling you to be careful, to go slow, or to back off. In sporting terms, it's the part of your brain that can cause resistance to making changes, even when change is clearly needed to allow you to achieve your full potential.

Here's an example of the lizard brain effect. At a soccer team training session, the coach suggests to a player that he should play in a different position. The player has the physical ability and skill to play in the new position but he resists the change. His resistance is not based on any 'real' concerns over his abilities, it's based on a past experience. He knows he's physically capable but he also knows that the last time he played in that position, it all went horribly wrong for the team and they were booed off the pitch by supporters at the end of the match. On one level, his rational, conscious thoughts tell him there's nothing to fear in the change of position, but  on another, subconscious level, there's an irrational nagging voice saying, "You can't play in that position. It'll all go wrong if you change positions."

That's the lizard brain response. The lizard brain doesn't like change. It *fears* change, and fear sabotages success.

Scientists believe our brains evolved in three stages. Our lizard brains are the ancient part, coping only with instinctive behavioural response patterns. The next stage, the mammalian brain, gave us an ability to file new experiences as they happened, effectively creating a store of experience-based memories. These memories could now influence current and future behaviour as the non-instinctive emotional responses of fear and anger emerged. In the third stage, the neocortex evolved, creating the human brain as we know it. Now we're able to draw on past experiences, sift through information, rationalise, and make conscious decisions on how to respond to situations using our intellect or our best judgement.

Well, that's the theory! But, in times of high stress and when the pressure is on, all of the theory is thrown out of the proverbial window and the lizard brain takes over. The ability to rationalise becomes lost and irrational thoughts creep to the forefront of your mind. Imagine for a moment that you're a racing car driver. You're having the race of your life; your car is performing brilliantly, and you too are firing on all cylinders, everything is going your way. Then, an opportunity to overtake presents itself; an opportunity for you to get into the lead. On a conscious level, the rational voice in your head says, "Go for it! You're all set up, make the move," but on a subconscious level, there's an irrational nagging voice saying, "Hold on! Make that move and you're doomed." That's your lizard brain response. Your 'new' brain, the neocortex, knows that you have been presented with a golden opportunity to succeed, but your 'old' brain, the lizard brain, knows that the last time you were in this position in a race, within a lap of taking the lead, your engine blew and you were out of the race. The pressure of once again being at the sharp-end of a race creates a 'fear factor' that effectively paralyzes you. Your lizard brain voice gets the Dolby-surround-sound treatment and any voice of reason is completely drowned out. You resort to survival mode - you don't take that 'chance'.

The tricky thing is, without our lizard brains, we'd be reckless in everything we did. A reckless soccer player probably wouldn't have made the team in the first place so a change of playing position wouldn't be on the cards and a reckless racing driver probably wouldn't have a very long racing career, or a very long life! But, the fear factor being generated by your lizard brain can be all that's holding you back and by holding back, you are unable to realise your full potential. The fear must be faced, no matter how imaginary or real that fear actually is, it's real to you. By confronting your fears, you are able to see each one through to its logical conclusion. You learn to approach stressful situations with the question: what's the worst thing that can happen? And, by seeing it through, you're able to realise that very often, the reality is nowhere near as bad as the fear would have you believe. Once a fear is faced, and accepted for what it is, steps can be taken to mitigate it.

Without a fear of change holding you back, you are free to give everything you do your very best effort and when you do, you will be compensated accordingly. You already know that you 'get out what you put in' and this Law is naturally connected to that principle. To receive the results you see in your vision of success, make sure that *all* of your efforts are focused on achieving that success.

> *"Good, better, best. Never let it rest, until your good*
> *is better and your better is best"*
> **- Tim Duncan, basketball player**

Ancient Way to Modern Day

Modern science and extensive research have led to a much greater understanding of human physiology and the effects of high intensity training on the body of a competitive athlete. In the 1970s, decathlete Daley Thompson was renowned for his strict training regime that saw him physically training every day, including Christmas Day; attitudes have since changed. World records continue to be broken and personal bests continue to be achieved because science allows us to continue pushing the limits of what may once have been believed impossible.

We recognise that less is sometimes more and it's not necessarily the quantity but the quality of effort that counts. In terms of total commitment to achieving more in sport, Greek philosopher Epictetus summed it up very succinctly when he said;

All philosophy in two words - sustain and abstain.

Law Seven

Like Attracts Like

Be a Magnet to Success

"Confidence is contagious. So is lack of confidence"
- Vince Lombardi, American football coach

Thinking positively leads to positive actions being taken and taking positive action leads to a positive outcome. This is an underlying message in all aspects of sports psychology and it's a concept that has been around for centuries, not least in ancient Greek and Chinese cultures where the 'healthy mind, healthy body' philosophy originated.

In **Law Two**, you learned that the positive energy you generate by thinking and acting positively is returned to you in the form of a positive vibe in a positive environment. The same basic principle is behind this Law. If you're sending out positive energy, you attract positive energy in return so by Law, if you're sending out negative energy, you attract only negative energy in return.

Franz Klammer used the extraordinary power of his own positive thinking to generate a positive vibe that overruled the negative thinking vibe of 60 000 spectators and turned their fearful gasps into a positive cheer of support that was no doubt ringing in his ears as he crossed the finish-line to win gold. The positive energy that he put out through thinking positively not only allowed him to ski positively, it was returned to him as a surge of positive energy from the spectators lining the course. His positive energy, attracted positive energy in return.

All of the Universal Laws link to the Universal Law of Attraction and all of the Laws covered in the chapters of this book link to this Law - Like Attracts Like. For example, Franz Klammer succeeded through his ability to maintain a positive mental attitude even when the odds seemed stacked against him but his ability to think positively didn't develop in isolation. His skills, both physical and mental, developed through his passion for his sport; his ability to visualise his success; his ability to create an action plan to achieve that success; his willingness to take action on that plan; his ability to create a positive outer world through maintaining a positive inner world; his dedication to putting in to his sport the necessary effort to get out the end result he wanted, and his commitment to always giving *everything* connected to his sport, his best effort. That adds up to a *lot* of positive thinking and a lot of positive action but in return for every positive effort, he attracted the positive things he needed to help him turn his vision of success into his reality. It's also important to recognise that winners like Klammer become winners because they're willing to lose. You have to be willing to lose in order to win because a fear of failure can only hold you back from giving your all and achieving a top performance.

EVERY POSITIVE EFFORT ATTRACTS A POSITIVE RETURN.

You know already that it takes a *total* commitment to your sport to realise your full potential. To attract positive outcomes, *all* of your thoughts and actions must be focused on achieving your ultimate goal, *all* of the time. All of the Laws of Performance link into this Law - Like Attracts Like - as achieving a top performance depends on your ability to attract the positive things into your life that will help you to be your best.

Of course, to continue performing at your best, you must continue to attract positive outcomes by continuing to think positively and continuing to take positive action: you must continue to give your all and maintain your total commitment to your sport. A great example of the effects of failing to maintain *total* commitment can be found in the story of Scotland's football team in the 1978 World Cup. In that year, every football fan in Scotland believed the Scottish team would win the World Cup in Argentina. If you're unfamiliar with Scotland's history in World Cup tournaments you'll find nothing unusual about a nation promoting themselves as winners in the build up to a big event, however, in previous campaigns, Scotland had made it almost a tradition to go out in the first round - if they even qualified to take part at all! So why was 1978 different?

In Scotland that year, it was impossible to escape the media frenzy that surrounded the Scottish team. They were touted as the greatest team in the history of British national teams - better than England's winning team of 1966 according to the Scottish press - and in sports psychology terms, the Scottish national team were being bombarded with positive external feedback from every source possible. The reason for the excitement was newly appointed manager Ally McLeod. It's reported that on introducing himself to the Scottish squad, he said, "My name is Ally McLeod and I'm a born winner." Soon after his appointment, he led Scotland to a British Home Championship win. He very quickly developed a team who believed themselves to be winners and in so doing, created an entire nation of believers. Thousands of supporters gathered to cheer on their team as they boarded the plane on their way to Argentina. The positive energy being generated by the team attracted positive energy in return from their enthusiastic supporters. One reporter asked McLeod what he planned to do after the World Cup. "Retain it," was his reply.

In 1978, sports psychology was not as widely recognised as it is today but what McLeod and the Scotland squad demonstrated was the phenomenal power of positive thinking: the power of a positive mental attitude. McLeod believed they would win, the players believed they would win, so an entire nation believed their team would win. As Scotland entered the World Cup, they were a perfect representation of the concept of positive thoughts leading to positive actions and positive actions leading to positive outcomes. However, Scotland lost their first match, drew their second, and were out of the World Cup by the end of the first round - again. What happened? Could it be that the team got so caught up in the positive thought part of the process that they forgot about the need to act? Did the media hype lead to them believing that all they had to do was show up and the trophy would be theirs? In McLeod's autobiography written the following year, he questions whether he, "generated just too much excitement" and wonders if he, "raised the level of national optimism just too high." McLeod and the 1978 Scotland squad may have failed to deliver the World Cup dream but what we can all learn from the enthusiasm generated by their campaign is that positive thinking holds real power. If the team had continued to take action and remained committed to *acting* positively as well as *thinking* positively, who knows what outcome they may have attracted in return.

POSITIVE ATTRACTION

Your outer world is a reflection of your inner world and tennis player Andy Murray is an interesting example of this principle in action. The happenings of your inner world attract corresponding happenings in your outer world.

Murray is commitment to sport personified. He has made a great many sacrifices to get to where he is now. At the age of only 15, he left his home in Scotland to train at a tennis academy in Barcelona. He knew then he wanted to pursue a professional career in tennis but it meant he and his family had to make a number of personal and financial sacrifices to get the best training possible. But, he is yet to realise his dream of winning a Grand Slam title. His commitment to his sport is total and he is, without question, a talented player. His positive efforts have attracted a great many positive outcomes so why is he yet to realise his ultimate vision of success?

Murray understands the strength of connection between his inner game and his outer game and he understands the power of self-belief and a positive mental attitude. After his defeat in Australia in 2009, he said in an interview, "If you don't expect to win, then when you get into a position to do so, you get scared. In Australia, I was the most disappointed I've ever felt. It was difficult to lose because I thought I was going to win. Some might be happy with a quarter-final or a semi but that's not my mentality." Clearly, he has the will to win and he believes in himself and his abilities but comments made by former Davis Cup captain John Lloyd indicate that the happenings in Murray's outer world - win or lose - are indeed a reflection of the happenings in his inner world, his mind. Lloyd's comment was:

"The problem has been the mental side of his game. He won't win unless he changes his attitude. He goes out there and looks like he does not want to be on the court...throwing away points and making lots of gestures to his support group. The top players on the Tour are predators. If they sense blood, they are going to go for it. When they see someone throwing out negative body language, it's like giving them a Christmas present! "

LIKE ATTRACTS LIKE. NEGATIVITY ATTRACTS NEGATIVITY.

Like attracts like but it's not just what you say that matters, it's what you believe and what you *do* that attracts positive outcomes.

In the 1998 Calgary Winter Olympics, an inspirational story of positive thinking and total commitment unfolded. The story of the first Jamaican bobsled team has since been given the Disney treatment in the film titled *Cool Runnings* but the true happenings of the event are testament to Walt Disney's belief that, "If you can dream it, you can do it." The four-man Jamaican team were undoubtedly the Olympic underdogs and had very little practical experience in terms of negotiating an actual bobsled track. The characters in the Disney version are seen getting to grips with the practicalities of the sport in everything from go-carts to bathtubs but in reality, their training had revolved around pushcart racing in Jamaica. On arrival in Alberta, they had to borrow spare sleds and equipment from other competing nations in order to be able to take part at all and it's fair to say that the arrival of a team from a tropical climate attracted a fair amount of not-so-positive media attention. However, in the true spirit of the Olympics and according to the Law of Like Attracts Like, the positive energy generated by the Jamaican team members attracted a positive return in the form of not only the equipment they needed but also the support and guidance of the other bobsledders.

The odds were stacked against them but their commitment was total. The sled driver committed himself totally to memorising every centimetre of the course. He knew every lump, bump and bend; he knew the exact speed they needed to negotiate every stage; and, most importantly, he knew how it needed to 'feel' to get it right. It made great Disney entertainment to view him sitting in the bathtub pretending to be going down the course but in fact, we were watching skilled visualisation in practice. Through their dedicated, positive efforts, they attracted a great many positive outcomes in the form of major improvements in practice sessions but, much to the disappointment of the massive crowd of supporters they had attracted into their lives, they failed to officially finish the course in competition after losing control of the sled and crashing. After the crash, the team members famously got out of the sled and walked it over the finish-line demonstrating total commitment to the end. The total support of the stunned spectators was made clear by the strength of the cheers and applause as the first Jamaican bobsled team crossed the finish. Not even Walt Disney could have dreamed of a more inspirational ending to the story! Before you can win a game, you have to not lose it. The Jamaican team didn't win their race but they certainly didn't lose it.

We are all connected. No one makes it to the top of their game on their own. To connect with the people and the things you need to help you achieve your dream, you need to attract them into your life by generating the positive energy that will bring them to you. Like attracts like.

Be your best, do your best, give your best
and you will attract the best.

Ancient Way to Modern Day

Recent research into the effects of optimism have strongly supported the principles behind the Universal Law of Attraction. Studies have concluded that optimists enjoy greater health in life, with one study of Harvard University students revealing that those with optimistic character traits at the age of 25 were significantly healthier at the ages of 45 and 60 compared to those who displayed pessimistic character traits.

Dr Martin Seligman of the University of Pennsylvania has studied sports teams for many years and has concluded that optimistic teams create greater positive synergy and perform better as a team compared to pessimistic teams. In a different study, athletes were led to believe that the result of a single performance was worse than it actually was. The following performances of the pessimistic athletes were negatively affected but those of the optimistic athletes were not. And in a retrospective study of healthy Hall of Fame baseball players who played between 1900 and 1950, it was found that the optimists had lived significantly longer.

Optimism is a common thread through proverbs and sayings from all around the world. One old Chinese proverb says;

Do not let those who say it cannot be done
get in the way of those who are doing it.

Law Eight

Without Change, Nothing Changes

Champions Embrace Change

"Face each day with the expectation of achieving good, rather than the dread of falling short"
- Shannon Miller, gymnast

Everything is energy and energy is constantly in motion. Your thoughts are energy and you know already that 'what you think, you become'. The Universal Law of Energy states that all energy in motion will eventually appear in a physical form so in other words, what you think about, you bring about. The principle behind this Law is that everyone has the capacity to change their circumstances by changing their thoughts.

YOU CAN CHANGE WHAT YOU BRING ABOUT BY CHANGING WHAT YOU THINK ABOUT.

If you don't like the way things are for you: if you don't like your 'lot' in life, you have the power to change your circumstances by changing how you think about things and changing how you do things. To make positive changes, you must change your focus away from the things you *don't* want and onto the things you *do* want. Your thoughts and actions must generate positive energy to receive positive outcomes in return.

In **Law Five**, you learned of the importance of developing a growth mindset and of accepting that change is always possible. Clearly, if you're not happy with your current level of performance, *not* changing will keep you right where you are. If you want to see a change in your performance, you have to *make* those changes by doing things differently. However, it's not always easy to make changes because even though you recognise that you *want* change, making changes means taking steps to move away from all that you're familiar with: it means stepping out of your safe, familiar, predictable comfort zone and into a world of unknowns. Your comfort zone can be a positive place if you learn to use it as a performance plateau - a place where you can pause for a moment and catch your breath; a place where you can take stock of your achievements so far and consider your options for the next leg of your journey towards your ultimate goal. But, if you use your comfort zone as a place to stop rather than pause, it becomes a negative place. When you stop in your comfort zone, it becomes a place to hide rather than a place to reflect and you effectively shut yourself off from all opportunities to discover your true potential. To be able to improve your performance and achieve more, you must be prepared to step out of your current comfort zone: you must be prepared to make changes.

CHANGE YOUR FOCUS FROM NEGATIVE TO POSITIVE TO EFFECT POSITIVE CHANGE.

If you fear change, you fear the unknown but in sport, the real fear is very often not just a fear of the unknown but an accompanying fear of failure. Fear can paralyze you and prevent you from making the changes you need to make progress. The negative energy generated through fear can also begin a self-perpetuating downward spiral of negative happenings. Remember the 'success cycle' when it began with a negative self-image? The positive cycle of success can also be viewed as a positive upward spiral, a spiral of success. The Zoned In Performance Spiral of Success™ programme[1] has been developed to promote awareness of the negative affects of fear in all areas of life and to promote positive ways to instigate change by changing the way you think to generate positive changes in your outcomes. If you think of the spiral of success as a spiral staircase, your comfort zone is at the very bottom of the stairs. If you fear change, facing the climb up those stairs feels like facing an experimental jet-pack flight wearing equipment supplied by Bodge-It-and-Scarper Inc. But, 'all great journeys begin with one small step' so all it takes to begin your upward journey is the confidence to take that first step.

The key to building confidence is to understand that you don't need to leap up the spiral of success in one enormous jump. You don't have to

---

1 Details of the Spiral of Success™ programme can be found on the Zoned In Performance website

change *everything* all at once. Changes can be made one small, manageable step at a time, just like climbing the steps of a spiral staircase. When you fear taking that first step, your lack of confidence has allowed negative 'what if?' questions to fill your mind - 'what if I'm not good enough: what if I fail?' Your negative thoughts generate negative energy and that negative energy can only generate a negative outcome which in this case means  you'll be stuck at the bottom of the stairs, unable to make any progress. The confidence to take that first step comes from changing your energy. The negative energy that's keeping you at the bottom of the stairs can be changed to positive energy by changing your thinking. Negative becomes positive simply by exchanging 'what if I fail?' with 'what if I succeed?' When you learn to think positively, 'what if I succeed?' becomes, 'I *can* succeed' and then 'I *will* succeed.'

Getting from the bottom of the spiral staircase to the top represents getting from 'what if?' to 'I will.' You're not going to jet-pack to the top, you're going to take one step at a time. Think of each step as a stepping-stone towards reaching your ultimate vision of success. Look at where you are now then change your focus to look ahead at where you want to be. Break the journey between the two points into small steps. Look at the skills you already have then consider the additional skills you will need to help you achieve your goal. The confidence you need to continue climbing up the stairs will come from developing those new skills. Success depends on having confidence in yourself and in your abilities. The building blocks of self-confidence are:

- Knowledge
Knowledge is power. Fear that is based on the unknown can be eliminated

through learning. With knowledge and preparation, confidence can be built.

- Skill

Identifying your own unique skills can be very empowering. Knowing your strengths gives you the confidence to tackle life's challenges.

- Experience

With experience comes knowledge. 'Learn from your mistakes' is a common saying but just as much can be learned from successes. Accomplishing goals builds confidence.

- Attitude

Your attitude is essential to your success. Believing that change is always possible allows you to remain optimistic through turbulent times.

- Self-belief

Your knowledge, skill, experience, and attitude create the foundation for self-confidence and belief in yourself. Believe, and have confidence, in your ability to take the next step.

Most of us, no matter how confident, experience moments of self-doubt. Each time you step out of your comfort zone, doubt can creep into your thoughts - 'Am I ready for this: can I do this?' Doubt stems from a lack of self-belief and could easily lead to a hasty retreat back into your comfort zone. Rather than stepping backwards, take a side-step. Take a moment to reflect on your achievements so far. Focus on your strengths while improving your weaknesses and give yourself credit where credit is due. Those nagging voices in your head are simply a sign that you're preparing to take the next step, you're getting ready to step out of your comfort zone. Nagging doubts are often accompanied by a feeling of butterflies in your stomach, another sign that you're getting ready to go. Silence the voices by telling yourself that you *are* ready, you *can* do it and then get those butterflies flying in formation - fly with them! You've worked hard and earned your right to make your way up the spiral of success; you *deserve* to be there.

Positive self-talk is an effective way of changing negative energy into positive energy. However, what you say must also be what you *believe*. For example, you might say, 'I'm going to improve my 10k running time' but what you *really* believe is, 'I'll never run 10k any faster than I do now.' Positive energy can only be generated by positive thoughts and they must be thoughts that your mind *believes* to be true. Only consistent thoughts can take physical form so if you've spent many years *believing* you'll never run any faster, deciding to say you'll run faster is not enough on its own to effect any sort of change. You must *believe* what you say and you must be consistent in what you think and what you say. Random thoughts or thoughts that are not congruent with long-held beliefs have no power.

In **Law Two**, you learned that the higher frequencies of positive energy can cancel out the lower frequencies of negative energy. The thoughts that you really believe in have far more power than the thoughts you're simply paying lip-service to! If you're thinking of a change you'd like to make but your real belief is 'it'll never happen,' your long-held belief is your dominant thought and negative thoughts can only manifest into negative outcomes. If you're not happy with what you're manifesting, you have to change your dominant thoughts; you have to focus on the things you want, not the things you don't want.

MAKING CHANGES

You know already that successful people have successful habits. Success is routine! It's a popular belief that it takes 30 days to form a new habit and the same applies to changing old habits. Habitual negative thinking will not transform into habitual positive thinking overnight.

> *"We are what we repeatedly do.*
> *Excellence, then, is not an act, but a habit"*
> **- Aristotle**

Commit to *thinking* positively and *believing* in your thoughts for a period of at least 30 days. Remember, it takes consistent positive thinking to achieve positive results and it takes total commitment to the task in hand to receive total payback in terms of success. Try the following:

- repeat positive affirmations and positive self-talk daily; believe what you say
- use visualisation to create a mental image of your success; believe what you see
- create a vision board; create a visible reminder of what your success looks like
- read inspirational quotes
- read positive books
- listen to positive music
- act as if you already have what you dream of; believe in yourself and your ability to *be* your vision of success and *be* the change you want to achieve
- be grateful for the good things you already have; reflect on your achievements so far and celebrate your successes.

GOALS ARE SET WITH THINKING AND RECEIVED WITH ACTION BUT YOU HAVE TO REALLY BELIEVE TO REALLY RECEIVE.

The first Jamaican bobsled team turned a potentially negative happening into a positive happening by pushing their crashed sled over the finish-line. Derek Redmond turned the negative energy of his hatred of everything, especially hamstrings, into the positive energy of his determination to finish the race he had started. They are inspirational examples of the power of positive thinking and of the principle behind this Law. Positive energy can and does cancel out negative energy. By changing your energy, you can change your outcomes.

Ancient Way to Modern Day

The Universal Law of Vibration states that everything in the universe creates its own unique vibration; its own frequency. Theoretical physicists openly discuss the 'string theory' which suggests that electrons and protons are all forms of vibration on tiny loops of string throughout the universe but 'mainstream' scientists are yet to back up any such theories, not because they are flawed but because they have no absolute proof - the theories behind the Law can't be tested.

Proven scientific theories have concluded that energy moves in circles - a pendulum returns in its swing, the moon returns in its orbit - but one man back in the early 1900s stated that because everything is energy and everything vibrates, even the vibrations of shares on the stock market could be predicted by applying the Natural Law of Vibration. His name was William D Gann and he did predict the exact points at which stocks and shares would sell with remarkable accuracy. He attributed his success solely to aligning himself with the Law of Vibration and he taught others how to do the same but his method has never been scientifically proven. His belief was that the Law of Vibration was fundamental to the invention of wireless telegraphy and the telephone.

Things only become possible once you believe they are possible. In 1954, scientists did not believe it was possible to run a sub-four-minute mile. Roger Bannister did it anyway! Before the invention of the telephone, how many people believed it was even a possibility?

Back in the 1600s, French poet Jean de la Fontaine said;

Man is so made that when anything fires his soul, impossibilities vanish.

Law Nine

Getting to the Top Means Getting Things in Perspective

Keep Your Performance in Perspective

"Treat a person as he is, and he will remain as he is. Treat him as he could be, and he will become what he should be"
- **Jimmy Johnson, American football coach**

How you define success and failure is a personal choice. In **Law Four,** you learned that the people and the things you attribute your success or failure to, in any given situation, give an insight into your emotional state. If you're in a competitive event where an official is keeping score, success and failure can easily be defined as the winner and the loser. But, how *you* define success or failure may not be so clear-cut. If your goal is to win the competition, you might view anything other than a win as outright failure but what if it's your goal to achieve a personal best and even though you lose the competition, you achieve a personal best? Is the end result now one of success or one of failure? Look at it another way, how do you define success or failure in a non-competitive situation? What constitutes success or failure in training?

It's a Universal Law that all things are relative. Everything is relative to something else. Something is only big in relation to something that's small; something is only fast in relation to something that's slow, so success and failure can only be relative to *your* perspective. The principle behind this Law is that nothing in life has any meaning except for the meaning we give it.

Nothing is big, small, fast or slow until you compare it to something else. If you're comparing yourself to others, you might feel that as the competition loser, you're a failure compared to the competition winner but consider this, the winner might also consider themselves to be a failure because they're comparing their winning score to someone-else's more impressive winning score! In any situation, how you define yourself or your circumstances is purely down to your perspective. From your perspective, the winner is successful but from the winner's perspective, they're unsuccessful. Success and failure don't exist: there really is no such thing as success or failure, only our *perceptions* of success and failure and our perceptions are all relative to our own beliefs.

Let's say you're a javelin thrower. You're in an Olympic qualifying round and you fail to make the required distance. You've failed, therefore you're a failure - or so *you* believe. You define yourself as a failure because you gave it your best shot but your best wasn't good enough. The other competitors' best's were better. Your comparison of yourself to others is negative. Your thinking is negative and your mental attitude is negative so you're generating negative energy. Negative energy will block your potential to progress from where you are now; you're stuck. However, all it would take to change your energy would be a change of perspective. Your best wasn't good enough today but tomorrow's best might be better. You failed to qualify but you succeeded in producing a season's best throw. In fact, the distance you threw today is the exact distance that one of the spectators dreams of achieving in their vision of success. From their perspective, you are a total success. To progress and to move on from the disappointment of today's result, you have to maintain a positive mental attitude and shift your focus away from what you *didn't* achieve and onto what you *did* achieve and what you still *can* achieve.

> **FOCUS ON THE POSITIVE THINGS YOU HAVE, RELATIVE TO WHAT OTHERS HAVE. FOCUS ON WHERE YOU SUCCEED BY COMPARISON, NOT ON WHERE YOU FAIL BY COMPARISON.**

Learning how to keep things in perspective is essential in terms of improving your performance and achieving your full potential. If it is your belief that your best throw today really was your absolute best and you're never going to be able to better it, you won't better it. If it is your belief that your best throw *today* was just that, your best throw *today*, but your absolute best throw is yet to come, it will come. Your ability to realise your full potential depends on your ability to keep things in perspective. When you're able to keep things in perspective, you're able to see that your best wasn't as good as someone else's best today but it was your best compared to your best throw last month, and last month's throw was your best throw compared to the previous month's best throw - your best just keeps on getting better!

British javelin thrower Steve Backley is a great example of keeping things in perspective. In the 2000 Sydney Olympics, he beat the qualifying mark with his first throw of 83.74 metres but rival Jan Zelezny threw an even bigger 89.39 metres to qualify convincingly. Unperturbed, Backley went on to throw a new Olympic record of 89.95 metres in the second round of the final, putting him in strong contention for the gold medal. However, in the third round, Zelezny threw a massive 90.17 metres which not only instantly broke Backley's record, it secured him the gold. Had Backley been unable to keep things in perspective, he may well have gone home that evening and cried into his Gatorade before hanging up his javelin and calling it a day. Instead, he began to prepare for the 2001 Athletics World Championships. As the event progressed, Backley was trailing behind the Latvian thrower's personal best of 86.47 metres and the American thrower's personal best of 85.91 metres. That's *two* rivals in the form of their lives, from anyone's perspective that's tough opposition. But, Backley responded by throwing 90.81 metres to take the gold medal.

> *"Success is a decision. Not a gift"*
> **- Steve Backley OBE**

Steve Backley won gold in four consecutive Commonwealth Games and medalled in three consecutive Olympic Games but never secured Olympic gold. From *your* perspective, is he a success or a failure?

**ONLY YOU CAN DECIDE HOW YOU VIEW YOUR CIRCUMSTANCES.
YOUR PERSPECTIVE IS YOUR CHOICE.**

Jim Abbott is a retired Major League baseball player who forged a successful career in sport despite having been born without a right hand. His ability to keep things in perspective is truly inspirational:

> *"There are millions of people out there ignoring disabilities and accomplishing incredible feats. I learned you can learn to do things differently, but do them just as well. I've learned that it's not the disability that defines you, it's how you deal with the challenges the disability presents you with. And I've learned that we have an obligation to the abilities we DO have, not the disability."*
> **- Jim Abbott**

When you are able to keep things in perspective, you are able to see the bigger picture. Your circumstances at any one moment in time are just that, one moment in time. You have the power to change your circumstances and to *keep* changing your circumstances; one moment in time does not define your entire career. Roger Federer, for example, did not just wake up one morning to find himself at the top of his game. Currently number two in the ATP men's tennis world rankings, he is the winner of 15 grand slam singles titles including five at Wimbledon. His rise to the top was not meteoric

and he experienced a great many defeats on his journey up through the ranks. In 1998, aged 17, Federer entered four ATP tournaments and lost three. Things weren't much better the following year, winning only one challenger event. Then in 2000, he lost five times in a row and totted up a total of 14 losses in first-round matches. I think it's fair to say that at this point many lesser mortals may have been considering a different career path, but he kept going: he saw the bigger picture and he kept things in perspective. In 2002, Andre Agassi beat Federer in a final. After the match, Agassi said, "When Roger Federer learns how to play tennis at this top level, we're all in trouble." And learn is exactly what Federer did. Improving his performance meant learning from his mistakes but *not* focusing on the failures; it meant learning from mistakes and *moving forward*. We all know that we can learn from mistakes but it's important to remember that we can also learn from successes. Federer's focus is never on the point or the game he's just lost, that moment is gone and can't be changed, it's always firmly on the points and the games he's still to win. He *knows* that he can change his circumstances in the very next moment, or the moment after that.

Things happen. With the best will in the world, things are not always going to go the way you planned. Seeing the bigger picture and keeping setbacks in perspective is the only way to keep moving forwards. Dwelling on negatives generates negative energy and negative energy can only hold you back.

POSITIVE PERSPECTIVES

In the 1928 Olympics, Australian sculler Bobby Pearce appeared unstoppable on his way to winning gold. His rowing prowess had been clearly demonstrated by his outstanding qualifying round times but an unusual event in his quarter-final literally *did* stop him:

"I had beaten a German and a Dane in earlier heats and I was racing a Frenchman when I heard wild roars from the crowd along the bank of the canal. I could see some spectators vigorously pointing to something behind me, in my path. I peeked over one shoulder and saw something I didn't like, for a family of ducks in single file was swimming slowly from shore to shore. It's funny now, but it wasn't at the time for I had to lean on my oars and

wait for a clear course, and all the while my opponent was pulling away to a five length lead."

Without the ability to keep things in perspective, the circumstances Pearce found himself in could have ended his medal chances. The negative energy created by his frustration at being stopped and his anger at seeing his opponent stretch his lead could have generated into such a negative environment that the race would effectively have been over. Dwelling on the negative experience of the race would then have led to Pearce beginning his next race with a negative attitude and still generating negative energy…and so the downward spiral would have continued. As it was, not only did he catch up, he crossed the finish line almost 30 seconds ahead of the Frenchman. He very definitely kept things in perspective! He knew that he was the faster rower; he knew that his qualifying times set him apart from his opponents, so he knew that he could still win the race and he channelled that positive energy into an all-out effort to do just that.

Keeping things in perspective means taking responsibility for yourself and for your circumstances. In **Law Five**, you learned that nothing happens by chance and that nothing happens out with the Universal Laws. That's not to say that a family of ducks crossing your path in a scull race isn't a chance happening but it does mean that the outcome of that happening is not a chance outcome. Your perspective; *your* attitude and *your* response to that happening is directly responsible for the outcome *you* generate. Win or lose, succeed or fail, it's all down to perspective.

Inspirational Perspectives

At the Nagano winter Olympics in 1998, Hermann 'Herminator' Maier was considered to be the best downhill skier in the world and touted as favourite to win every event he competed in. On his downhill run, travelling in excess of 70 mph, he attempted to turn left on an icy bend.

His skis didn't catch the snow and he flew, literally, off the course. High winds had already forced an alteration to the course and they now picked him up and hurled him through the air before dropping him onto the course to begin a 50 yard tumble into some safety netting. The crowd held their breath - he must be dead. In fact, he stood up and walked off the course!

The Herminator suffered injuries to his shoulder and knee but over the next few days he demonstrated his own brand of inner strength and showed his remarkable perspective on life by not only returning to the slopes, but dominating them by winning gold in both the super G and giant slalom. From his perspective, he wasn't dead and he was still able to ski, therefore he could still compete. He took responsibility for what had happened, he focused on the positives, and he moved on.

Ancient Way to Modern Day

The principle behind this Universal Law correlates with Albert Einstein's Theory of Relativity. Einstein's theories are not always easy to grasp but this theory, proposed in the early part of the 20th century, has stood the test of time and been confirmed accurate under the scrutiny of a great many other scientists over the years. Einstein said;

Reality is merely an illusion, albeit a very persistent one.

The need to keep things in perspective is a lesson that has been passed down through countless generations with pearls of wisdom such as, "There's always someone worse off than yourself," and the importance of focusing on the positives that you have in life are perhaps best expressed by the wise words of Buddha who said;

Let us rise up and be thankful, for if we didn't learn a lot today, at least we learned a little, and if we didn't learn a little, at least we didn't get sick, and if we got sick, at least we didn't die; so, let us all be thankful.

Law Ten

You Win Some, You Lose Some

You Have to Know Failure to Know Success

"No matter how good you are, you're going to lose one-third of your games. No matter how bad you are, you're going to win one-third of your games. It's the other third that makes the difference."

- **Tommy Lasorda, Major League baseball player and manager**

You already know there's no such thing as success or failure, only your perception of success or failure and only in comparison to other things. It's a Universal Law that everything has an opposite and without those opposites, neither one would exist. So, for example, if there was no good, there would be no bad; if there was no fast, there would be no slow, and if there was no success, there would be no failure.

The principle behind this Law is that success is only possible because of failure. If it was impossible to fail, it would be impossible to succeed. This doesn't mean that you *have* to fail in order to succeed, it means that you have to accept the possibility of failure in order to realise success or that to be willing to win also means being willing to lose. It means understanding that failure is only one end of a spectrum with success at the opposite end. And, crucially, it means accepting that you are responsible for your positioning in the spectrum and that you have the power to change that positioning by applying **Law Nine** and **Law Eight** at any time.

Think of it this way: if you currently see yourself as a failure, what you're experiencing is your perception of failure but failure can only exist because success also exists. This means that your perception of failure is based purely on your perception of success. Wherever you see yourself, your current position is your current perspective. By changing your perspective, you can change your position. Remember, your perspective is your choice.

> **YOU CAN ONLY EXPERIENCE A BAD DAY IF YOU HAVE ALSO EXPERIENCED A GOOD DAY.**
> **IF THERE WERE NO BAD DAYS, THERE WOULD BE NO GOOD DAYS!**

If you can see yourself as a success: if you have a clear vision of your success, you can apply the contents of this book to your current positioning on the spectrum to progress from where you are now to where you want to be.

Let's say you view your current level of performance as fairly average. You don't see yourself as a failure but you don't see yourself as the success you want to be either. You know that you must make changes because you know that not making changes will keep you where you are, in the average category. But, you fear change because you fear failure. So, here's a thought; if you fear failure you must also fear success!

YOUR SUCCESS OR YOUR FAILURE IS CONTROLLED BY YOU.

Fear paralyzes you, you're stuck where you are. To be able to move towards success, you must *move*. To move, you must overcome your fear and this means building your confidence.

dictionary definition of confidence -
- the belief that one can have faith in or rely on someone or something.
alternative definition of confidence -
- a state of mind; a reflection of your thinking.

In sport, confidence is self-belief: an unshakeable belief in yourself and in your capabilities. Building that confidence can begin by building your skill set with an understanding of the 'Four Pillars of Performance'.

PILLARS OF PERFORMANCE

There are four recognised pillars on which all great sporting performances rest. Those pillars, just like structural pillars supporting a building, must share the weight of their load evenly if the whole structure is to stay standing. Whether you are a coach or a player, think of the pillars of performance as columns of ability; if your ability in one area has grown more than in another, you will have an uneven load and your overall performance may begin to show signs of structural stress and start to crumble. The four pillars of performance are:

Technical

What technical skills are needed in your sport? As an athlete or player, an understanding of the technical requirements of your sport is essential if you are to achieve a top class performance. The same level of understanding is a must for any coach aiming to guide an athlete towards a winning performance, making it important to ensure your technical ability always matches the requirements of your athletes or players. As their skills and abilities increase, so must yours.

Tactical

Some sports are considered more tacti-cal than others. Team sports such as soc-cer and rugby are good examples but all sports, even solo events, have tactical elements that can make the difference between a mediocre performance or a winning one. As a player, you need game tactics in place long before the start of the match and as an athlete, you need race tactics in place long before you hear the starter's gun so as a coach, an abil-ity to discuss and plan the 'best' tactics for each new situation is vital. Changing

conditions, different competitors, and changing abilities may all require a change of tactics.

Physical

It's fair to say that a professional soccer player is generally fitter than a professional darts player and it's also fair to say that a professional soccer coach doesn't need to be as fit as his players to be a good coach but, whatever your sport and whatever role you play, you must be 'fit for purpose'. Being fit enough to run a marathon doesn't mean you're physically prepared to compete in the triple-jump. Without an understanding of how the human body adapts to physical training and how to apply a progressive programme of fitness training, optimum fitness for each sport is unlikely to be achieved.

Psychological

When all other elements are equal - technical, tactical, and physical abilities - what is it that makes one player win over another? The answer is often mental skill; the ability to remain focused when it really counts or, as many successful players refer to it, the winning 'edge'. Top performers, both athletes and coaches, recognise the importance of the mind-body connection and place equal emphasis on mental skills training and physical skills training.

As an athlete or player, identifying where your weaknesses are is the first step towards allowing yourself to grow as a performer. To be able to play to your strengths, you must know what they are. The key to greater success is then to develop your weaker skills, rather than hiding from them, so they match your existing strengths. This will not only correct the imbalance in your supporting pillars but will allow you to build onwards and upwards. Building your skills builds your confidence and with growing confidence you learn to overcome your fears, and realise that there are no limits to what you're capable of, other than the limits you place on yourself.

> *"Everyone needs something to believe in, and I believed in myself"*
> **- Muhammad Ali, heavyweight boxing champion**

The more skilled you become at visualising your success, the more familiar you become with what success looks like for you. Familiarity with success is a good thing as familiarity removes the fear of the unknown. Removing that fear allows you to move. Visualisation is key to success in the game of golf. If you watch professional golfers in action, preparing to take a shot involves not only physical preparation in terms of achieving the correct stance and grip on the club, it involves mental preparation in terms of achieving the correct degree of focus and then visualising where they want the ball to go *before* they swing their club. If you can see yourself playing a successful golf shot in your mind's-eye, you know what you have to do to play that successful shot in reality. It's exactly the same in any sport. If you have a vision of your success, you can take steps to achieve that success.

Not every shot you play on the golf course is going to go exactly where you aimed it. In any sport, things aren't always going to go your way but with a positive mental attitude, setbacks can be kept in perspective. Playing a shot straight into the middle of the water hazard wasn't part of your game plan but it's not the end of your game either. You just have to play your next shot from where your ball landed and get yourself back on course. By keeping a positive attitude, you can learn from the experience and move forwards. By Law, bad shots only exist because of good shots so to get that good shot, you have to keep taking another shot.

> *"You miss 100 per cent of the shots you never take"*
> **- Wayne Gretzky, ice hockey player**

Golf is not about getting a hole in one, it's about playing 18 holes and keeping score with 'old man par'. In golf, you don't need to have a perfect score at each hole you play, it's your score at the end of all 18 holes of play that counts. Experienced golfers think of a golf course as eighteen separate sections. Each section, or hole played, represents a step towards successful completion of the whole course. The ultimate goal is to complete the course; each hole played is a stepping-stone goal towards achieving that goal, and specific goals are set to boost the chances of successfully completing each stepping-stone goal. So, for example, a golfer preparing to play the first hole on the course might set himself the target of completing the task in five shots. He must now visualise where each one of those shots will take his ball in order to make sure that the fifth shot sees his ball sinking into the hole on the green. With a clear vision of where he wants the ball to land after his first swing, he's now mentally prepared to play that shot. Let's say he has visualised his first shot taking the ball 50 yards in a straight line to land in the centre of the fairway, avoiding rough grass and trees on the right and a bunker on the left. After taking his shot, he profiles it. In others words, he watches the ball in flight and studies its path. Profiling a shot allows a golfer to analyse whether the actual shot matches the visualised shot. If not, he's in a good position to figure out *why* not and adjustments can then be made.

> ## IF YOU PERCEIVE A SHOT TO BE SLIDING YOU TOWARDS THE FAILURE END OF THE SPECTRUM THEN YOU HAVE THE POWER TO MAKE THE NEXT SHOT SLIDE YOU THE OTHER WAY - BOTH ENDS OF THE SPECTRUM EXIST.

If the golfer's shot landed his ball in the trees instead of on the fairway, it's not 'game over'. He must now carry on making his way around the course from where he is now: he must visualise where he wants the ball to land after his next shot. It might not be the route he originally planned to reach the first green but it doesn't mean he can't get there. This principle can be applied to all sports. There's no guarantee that every step you map out for yourself on your action plan is going to bring you exactly the result you were aiming for but it doesn't mean you have to stop. You keep going, you keep moving forward. You might need to take a detour but you *can* still get to where you want to go. If you stop moving, you're going nowhere.

In **Law Eight**, you learned about the spiral of success and how a fear of stepping out of your comfort zone can keep you stuck at the bottom. To a golfer, each hole of play represents another step on the spiral staircase. They have to keep playing to get to the 18th green so they have to keep taking those steps one-by-one. Before they take a step, they visualise what that step represents in terms of their positioning on the golf course and their score. After each step they take, they profile it. If their reality doesn't match their vision, it doesn't mean they have to go back down to the bottom of the stairs, they carry on from where they are. They might take a side-step to analyse their current position but they will then plan their next step by looking at where they want to go from where they are *now*.

Getting from where you are now to where you want to be in your sport can only happen if you're prepared to take steps to get there. To get anywhere, you have to move. Until you move, you're going nowhere. Making that move towards success means accepting that not every step you take is going to take you in exactly the direction you planned. To accept success, you must also accept failure. You can always take another step so you can always get back on track.

> *"My motto was always to keep swinging. Whether I was in a slump or feeling badly or having trouble off the field, the only thing to do was keep swinging"*
> **- Hank Aaron, baseball player**

Ancient Way to Modern Day

The principle behind this Law links to the science behind the theory of polarity. Everything has an opposite and one end of a spectrum can't exist without the other. It's a concept that is used in hypnosis as negative or undesirable thoughts can be suppressed by concentrating on the opposite; negative beliefs can be replaced by positive beliefs.

The Chinese Yin-Yang symbol is an ancient example of the Natural Law of Polarity. In Chinese culture it's believed that everything has masculine (yang) and feminine (yin) principles and that they are the basis of all creation.

When you apply this Law to your life, you accept that in every situation, no matter how bad, there will also be good - you just have to look for it. This is a sentiment shared by an ancient Maori proverb that says;

Turn your face to the sun and the shadows fall behind you.

Law Eleven

The Only Way Is Up...Down...Up...
Accept the Rough With the Smooth

"Success is never permanent and failure is never final"
- **Mike Ditka, American football player and coach**

You now know that everything in the world is energy and everything, in both your inner and outer world, is constantly moving and vibrating. Your thoughts as well as your actions create their own unique vibrations and attract similar vibrations in return. When you're thinking positively, you attract positive energy so by Law, when you're thinking negatively, you attract negative energy. The principle behind this Law is that the energy you generate is not only constantly moving, it constantly moves in natural cycles.

It's a Universal Law that everything has a natural rhythm and that there is a time and a season for *everything*. When you're able to understand and accept that everything moves in cycles, you're able to remain positive during the negative phase of a cycle, knowing that what goes around, comes around. You learned in the last chapter that everything has an opposite so where there's a negative, there must also be a positive. By understanding the natural cycle, you're able to ride out bad days, *knowing* that good days are on their way.

Everything has a natural cycle and sport is no exception. In nature, the natural cycle revolves around the seasons and a number of sports also revolve around their own seasons. As an athlete or player, it's your goal to reach peak fitness at the peak of your sport's season but it's simply not possible to remain at your peak all year round. Whatever your sport, your fitness training programme is effectively a training cycle. Reaching your peak physically is only possible through following a progressive training plan that includes not only periods of intense exercise but also appropriate periods of rest and recovery. Ignoring the natural cycle

increases the risk of suffering an injury but even when following the most meticulous of training plans, accidents and injuries can still occur.

When your life revolves around your sport, an injury at any point in your training cycle can be a source of extreme frustration. However, *everything works in natural cycles, including injury recovery.* If you allow your frustration to dominate your thoughts and your actions, the negative energy you generate will only prolong the recovery process.

The emotional effects of long-term sports injury rehabilitation have been likened to the recognised 'Five Stages of Grief'.

ONE - Denial
Especially at elite level, a sportsperson considers themselves to be 'superior' in terms of physical strength - it's just not possible that they could be injured.

TWO - Anger
The realisation that they are injured leads to anger; a period of being angry at themselves for having allowed the injury to occur.

THREE - Bargaining
At this stage, an injured athlete will try desperately to speed up their return to play by attempting to bargain with absolutely everyone. They'll plead with the physio, the coach, and passers-by in the street to be able to return to training - "if I do this exercise for a whole week, can I try playing next week?"

FOUR - Depression
As the weeks of enforced rest continue, a player begins to feel sorry for themselves and can become increasingly withdrawn as they feel out of sorts with life. It's at this stage, a player might lose hope of ever fully recovering and give up on their sport completely.

FIVE - Acceptance
At this final stage of acceptance, a player realises that focusing on the physical rehabilitation process is the way forward.

Progressing from 'depression' to 'acceptance' is a natural cycle but reaching the stage of being able to accept that the road to recovery is to focus on the physical rehabilitation plan is a process that can be shortened by also accepting this Law. Your injury is your reality and no matter how much you try to deny it or how angry you feel about it, the fact that you are injured remains unchanged. You can't change what has already happened but you *can* change what happens next. Anger, frustration, and negative thinking can only ever hold you back. To move forwards, and in this case to recover, you must generate positive energy by focusing on what you have yet to achieve and still *can* achieve. The injury was not part of your action plan but it does not represent the end of the road. Everything has an opposite and everything moves in cycles so where there is injury there will also be recovery.

Without bad days there would be no good days, without lows there would be no highs. Your injury represents a low but it's a low that's part of a cycle and the cycle will return you to a high. To limit the time you spend at the low end of the cycle, you must maintain a positive mental attitude and continue to generate the positive energy that will speed your recovery.

THE FASTEST ROUTE BETWEEN TWO POINTS IS THE PATH OF LEAST RESISTANCE.

The fastest route from injury to recovery is to accept the natural cycle of energy that exists between the two points and to go with the flow. The more you resist the natural cycle of recovery, the more you prolong the process. Resistance becomes like swimming against the tide. When you swim against the tide, you run the risk of using a great deal of energy to find you've made very little, if any, progress. The fastest way to move in or out from the shore is to let the tide carry you. The tide will always turn.

Attempting to maintain peak physical fitness without allowing your body adequate rest and recovery time is also an attempt to resist the natural Law. Prolonged periods of physical stress can lead to injury but when combined with prolonged periods of psychological stress, the end result is often burnout. In a sports environment it's easy to see where the sources of physical stress are but sources of psychological stress can be more difficult to recognise. Psychological stress occurs when perceived demands, threats or fears outweigh the perceived capabilities or benefits. What this actually means, in terms of competitive sport, is that you begin to feel threatened, rather than challenged, by your environment and other competitors. At best, burnout will have a de-motivating effect on your performance but at worst, it can lead to giving up on your sport completely.

Of course, not all stress is 'bad' and a degree of stress is essential in sport to motivate you to perform well. Competitive stress experienced on a competition day can usually be considered as 'good' stress and a normal part of the preparation process. The more experienced you become as a competitor, the more you learn to monitor and control the amount of stress you are feeling, making it possible to get into your zone - your zone of optimal functioning. However, just as repeated physical stress can result in injury, repeated psychological stress can lead to good stress becoming bad stress. Remember, if there was no bad, there would be no good, and *all* things move in cycles, the good and bad energies of competitive stress included. The good stress that once motivated you and elevated you into your zone can become de-motivating bad stress, indicating you're close to, or already, experiencing burnout.

TO AVOID, OR RECOVER, FROM BURNOUT -

- understand the nature of stress and burnout

- take a look at the demands being placed upon you
- take the time to evaluate your capabilities in terms of meeting those demands
- learn a relaxation technique such as visualisation, centering or deep breathing
- develop mental training skills alongside physical skills to increase your ability to deal with the demands
- use goal setting to help keep motivation high in all areas of your life
- adopt or maintain a healthy lifestyle
- understand and accept the cyclical nature of all energy and that you can change the happenings of your outer world, your reality, by changing the happenings of your inner world, your mind.

Positive energy generates positive outcomes. Going with the flow and accepting that lows can and will return to highs is a powerful way to maintain a positive mental attitude and to continue generating positive energy. Remember, the tide always turns: *you* have the power to change *your* energy and a number of sporting greats are testament to the principle behind this Law. If what goes up must come down, then what goes down must also go up.

Inspirational Comebacks

Road Cycling
Lance Armstrong, seven times winner of the Tour de France, had already established a successful career in cycling when in 1996 at the age of 25 he was diagnosed with stage three testicular cancer. The cancer spread to his lungs, abdomen, and brain, and the surgeon who removed the testicular tumour stated at the time that Armstrong had less than a 40 per cent chance of survival. He received his last chemotherapy session in December 1996 and by January of 1998 he was already back on his bike

and in serious training. In 1999, he won the Tour de France for the first time and the rest, as the saying goes, is now inspirational sports history.

Golf

Hall of Fame golfer Ben Hogan is considered to be one of the all-time greatest golf players in the history of the game. In 1949, at the age of 36 and at the height of his career, he was in a car accident that left him with a double-fracture of the pelvis, a fractured collar bone, a left ankle fracture, and near-fatal blood clots. At the time, his doctors said that he may never walk again, let alone play competitive golf. He left hospital 59 days after the accident. In 1953, he won five of the six tournaments he entered and the first three major championships of the year - a feat now known as the 'Hogan Slam'.

Ancient Way to Modern Day

Known science has proved that everything in the universe is energy and energy moves in cycles and this adds weight to the principle behind the Universal Law of Rhythm. We know that the tide goes in and out, that planets are in orbit, and that for something to sink, something else must rise. The same applies to the Law of Rhythm; the sun rises and sets, the seasons change, and so does our emotional state. No one is happy all the time, and, according to Einstein's Theory of Relativity, it's only possible to know happiness if you also know sadness!

The importance of accepting the natural cycle of everything in life and going with the flow is a key message in a great many old sayings, including the French proverb which states;

Every flow has its ebb.

Law Twelve

Champions Recognise the Champion Within

Believe in Yourself as a Champion

"Mind is everything: muscle - pieces of rubber. All that I am, I am because of my mind"
- Paavo Numi, Olympic athlete

If you're familiar with the saying, "As sure as eggs is eggs," you'll know that it's used to describe something that's certain; something that is beyond any shadow of doubt. So, in the world of sport, is it possible to be certain of anything: if it's your ambition to become a sports champion, is it possible to be certain that you will become that champion?

The ancient Universal Laws *and* modern sports psychology tell us that something we can all be absolutely certain of is that we all have the power within us to be masters of our own destiny. As sure as eggs is eggs, we are all who we believe ourselves to be and our circumstances are simply a reflection of who we believe we are. To become a sports champion, you must *believe* that there is a sports champion within you. Without that inner belief, the only thing you can be absolutely certain of is that you will *not* become that champion.

> **CHAMPIONS BECOME CHAMPIONS FROM WITHIN: CHAMPIONS KNOW WHO THEY ARE AND THEY KNOW WHO THEY WANT TO BE. THEY RECOGNISE THAT GETTING TO THE TOP OF THEIR SPORT WILL TAKE DEDICATED EFFORT BUT THEY FOCUS ALL OF THEIR ENERGY INTO PRACTICING THE PHYSICAL AND MENTAL SKILLS THEY NEED TO BECOME THE BEST THEY CAN BE.**

If you ask any youngster keenly involved in sport about their sporting aspirations, they'll invariably tell you that they want to become a champion. In fact, they'll confidently tell you that they **are going to be** a champion. We already know that achieving an ambition is only possible once you believe it's possible, so will the youthful self-confidence and 'I'm invincible' attitude of aspiring young champions be enough to take them to the top of their sport, or is there something more? Young athletes love to emulate the champions of their sport and they may aspire to become just like them, but the ones who will go on to become champions themselves are the ones who, first and foremost, just love to take part in their sport. The 'something more' is nothing more than an undying *want* to be involved.

> *"If you're a champion, you have to have it in your heart"*
> **- Chris Evert, tennis champion**

Getting to the top of your game is going to take dedicated training. It's always going to be easier to do what you *want* to do, rather than something you should do or *have* to do. The heart of a champion is in their sport. Champions do what they love and they love what they do. Many of today's champion athletes tell stories of their childhood and of how they *knew* they wanted to become a champion from a young age. They might use the words "driven" or "compelled" to describe their feelings and their attitude towards succeeding in sport and they almost always refer to the

fact that the "buzz" they first felt through taking part in their sport has never left them. That's the key to success right there: win or lose, the motivation to keep playing remains the same.

SUCCESS IS A JOURNEY, NOT A DESTINATION.

Rafer Johnson is a former decathlete and Olympic champion. He advises young athletes with words of wisdom from personal experience. "What I can tell them is the way you become an Olympic champion is to start working now. I tell them why it's always worth it to put the time and effort into something you want to be good at." To "start working now" means realising that setting the goal of becoming an Olympic champion is only the beginning. Successful people have successful habits so you must develop the habits of thinking and acting successfully - starting now. What *you* **think** on a daily basis and what *you* **do** on a daily basis will ultimately decide *your* level of success. Every thought and every action you take on a daily basis must represent another step towards achieving your goal.

> ## CHAMPIONS ARE MADE, NOT BORN: THE POWER TO *MAKE* A CHAMPION IS INSIDE YOU.

Make sure that what you think you want to achieve is really what you want to achieve and that what you're doing is really what you want to do. Commit to *your* goals and make every thought and every action, in training and in competition, count.

CHAMPION'S CHOICE

There are times that before you can fully commit to a goal, you must make a choice. Let's say you are a multi-talented sports player. You are a world class performer in two or more sports and you must now decide which one sport to focus on in order to move forwards into a professional sports career. How do you make that decision?

It's often said that decisions are made by 'head' or by 'heart' which suggests that the process of making a decision must be either one or the other; a clinical, calculated process of choosing the option you 'think' is right or a more instinctive, emotional process of choosing the option that 'feels' right. So, using head or heart, what makes a decision the *right* decision?

The bottom line is, you can't know the outcome of any decision you make until after you make it, so, in effect, there's no such thing as a 'right' or 'wrong' decision. Of course, if things don't then turn out the way you planned, you believe the decision you made to have been the wrong one, but what's to say that swinging your decision the other way at the time of making it would have created the outcome you planned? You can't 'know' if you've made the 'right' decision until after the event, or can you?

Put yourself back in the shoes of that multi-talented sports player for a moment. The decision you must make is monumental; your decision is going to affect the whole of the rest of your life and you can't decide what to do for the 'best'. But here's the thing, if you know what it is you *really* want to achieve, chances are you *already know* which decision will give you the greatest potential to achieve it.

> **THE MORE YOU *REALLY* WANT TO DO SOMETHING, THE MORE LIKELY IT IS THAT YOU WILL.**

Look at it this way; if you *really* can't decide between two sports, then a simple coin toss is going to be as good a way as any to have the decision made for you, right? Heads for one, tails for the other. Go ahead and flip a coin - how does the call make you feel? Your thoughts and emotions as you watch the coin spin will provide you with the answer to the question of what you *really* want.

In the majority of cases, we already know which decision represents what we *really* want to do so why do we then continue to agonise over which decision is the 'right' decision? Well, if you're the multi-talented sports player, the answer to that question is that you've allowed that one decision to become much more monumental than it actually is. Decisions become much easier to make when you remember that any one decision you make does not in itself decide the outcome of the rest of your life.

Which sport should I focus on: which training schedule should I follow: which dietary advice should I follow: which lucky socks should I wear on competition day: should I wash my lucky socks or not...?

With the benefit of hindsight, you may come to realise that the option you chose did not lead to the outcome you wanted but that doesn't mean you're out of options. The outcome of the rest of your life is the result of countless decisions; is any one decision really that important?

As a multi-talented player, every one of your coaches will provide you with a list of reasons why you should focus on their particular sport but remember this, *should do* is never as powerful or as motivational as *want to do*. A sports player without motivation will never realise their true potential so the decisions you make must be *yours*. Agonising over decisions only serves to sap your energy so learn to go with what you already *know*. Know what you want to achieve, know what motivates you to achieve it, and you already know which decision represents the 'right' decision for you.

TRY SUBSTITUTING THE WORD 'DECISION' WITH THE WORD 'CHOICE'.

We make hundreds of choices in an average day and we don't waste time and energy agonising over every single one: which underwear will I wear today; jam or marmalade on my toast; coffee or tea - you get the idea? You make choices instinctively and you have the same power within you to make decisions. Don't get stuck under 'weighty' decisions, make a choice. Think of it this way; if you choose coffee, it doesn't mean you can't choose tea next time.

The ancient wisdom of the Universal Laws is an inner wisdom that's within us all, it just might be hidden under the clutter of modern living and the pressures of modern competitive sport. To improve your performance and to step up your game to the next level, take time out to reconnect with who you are and why you chose to be involved in your sport. Remember, successful people do what they love and love what they do. Do you love what you do?

CHOOSE CHOICE

When you find your passion, you find your inspiration, and when your performance is inspired, you find your success. Take a look at Martin's story:

Martin is an amateur triathlete. He's an exceptional cyclist, a competent runner, and a fairly average swimmer. He's a consistent performer in competitive events, rarely finishing out of the top five but he's yet to secure a win. His goal for the coming season is to be a winner.

Training for triathlon events is time consuming but Martin has found the perfect way to build his base fitness by alternating between cycling and running to and from work. Swimming, however, is proving more difficult. The best time of day for lane swimming at his local pool is early in  the morning but Martin's attempts to establish a regular training pattern of swimming on the way to work have so far failed to become a routine habit. The 'routine' of cycling or running to and from work has become such an established pattern of behaviour that it's now a habit. When things become habit, you're doing them without thinking about them - like brushing your teeth. Martin doesn't wake up in the morning and think about whether he can be bothered to cycle his favourite two hour route into work or not, he just does it: he doesn't have to wake up and decide whether or not to run his favourite hour route into work, there's no decision to be made, it's just what he does. So why is it proving difficult to *just swim*? The answer is that things don't become habit overnight; habits are formed over time.

Martin has formed the habit of cycling and running to work so why can't he simply form the habit of swimming? The answer; motivation. Martin was motivated to cycle to work because he wanted to boost his cycling fitness for triathlon and commuting to work represented a time-efficient way to do it. It was a choice: Martin *chose* to commute by bike. What's key about his choice is that he knew it was just that, a *choice*. His decision to cycle into work didn't represent his one and only opportunity to make a choice, he knew he always had the option to choose again and perhaps choose *not* to cycle into work. His choice provided a positive outcome - early morning air, less traffic, positive 'buzz' for the day ahead - which led to choosing to do it again, and then again, until it became a routine habit. The more he cycled, the fitter he became and the more he enjoyed it: he became an exceptional cyclist because he routinely cycled.

His motivation to swim is the same. Martin knows he needs to put in more practice time in the pool to improve his swimming fitness for triathlon but the habit of swimming on the way to work has yet to be formed, why? The outcome of his swimming experiences has not provided the same degree of motivation to continue. He chose to go swimming on the way to work but on subsequent occasions he has chosen not to swim on the way to work. So is it simply that he doesn't enjoy swimming? Well, here's the thing; Martin *did* enjoy swimming until he made the decision to *improve* his swimming. He enjoyed the weekly triathlon club training night at the local pool but his standard of swimming did not match that of his cycling and running so he made the decision to do more. He downloaded the 'Swim-like-an-Olympian' training schedule created by the BustAGut Training Corp. and plotted the suggested training targets in his training diary. Motivation was high. However, the training targets were completely unrealistic for a non-professional athlete. Martin's failure to reach even the first one was totally de-motivating. So much so that he sometimes chose not to go to the weekly triathlon club swimming session. His efforts to swim more resulted in swimming less.

Doing things you *want* to do is always going to be easier than doing things you feel you *have* to do or *should* do. For Martin, cycling and running are clearly things he *wants* to do. Improving his swimming is also something he *wants* to do because, ultimately, he wants to win a triathlon. He *wants* to win, but does he *have* to? He wants to improve his swimming but does he have to 'Swim-like-an-Olympian' to succeed? Putting unrealistic pressure on yourself or having someone else put that pressure on you, a coach for example, can actually defeat the object. Attempting to achieve too much can lead to achieving very little, or nothing at all.

Not *having* to win a triathlon does not mean that Martin should give up on his goal of *wanting* to win one. It means recognising that wanting to win a triathlon is a choice. Cycling and running to work are choices, whether or not to go to the swimming pool is a choice, so the key to success is to make successful choices. In Martin's case, the BustAGut Corp. training schedule did not represent a successful choice but it must be recognised as just a *choice* and not the end of the road. Martin's next choice is to swim at the weekly club session and then to commit to swimming with club members on two other arranged swims each week. Swimming with others is something he *wants* to do. He has made a choice that will allow him to enjoy his journey to success.

As sure as eggs is eggs, you *can* become whatever *you* put *your* mind to, and as sure as eggs is eggs, getting to the top of your game is going to take dedicated effort. Find your passion, believe in yourself as a champion, and then give it your all by applying your mind, your body, and your soul. Enjoy your journey.

> *"Greatness is earned, never awarded"*
> **- Nike**

Ancient Way to Modern Day

Studies related to modern sports science and sports psychology have produced convincing evidence to support this Law. The 'winning edge' in competitive sport is effectively a psychological edge or in other words, an unshakeable self-belief.

Winners in sport believe in themselves as winners and it's a belief that may be held long before the physical ability to become a winner has been developed. Heavyweight boxing legend Muhammad Ali is a powerful example of this principle in action. He is famed for his, "I am the greatest" statement but he also said, "I am the greatest. I said that even before I knew I was."

Indian philosopher Mahatma Ghandi perhaps explained it best when he said;

If I have the belief that I can do it, I shall surely acquire the capacity to do it even if I may not have it at the beginning.

The 12 Hidden Laws
of Performance
In Summary

A TOP PERFORMANCE IS AN INSPIRED PERFORMANCE
No one makes it to the top in sport on their own. We are all connected and we all have the capacity to both inspire and be inspired. Find your inspiration and you find your success.

> *"The best and fastest way to learn a sport is to watch and imitate a champion"*
> **- Jean-Claude Killy, Alpine ski racer**

POSITIVE THOUGHTS GENERATE POSITIVE OUTCOMES
Everything is energy and energy vibrates. Your thoughts, your actions, and your beliefs all generate their own energy so you have within you the power to create your own positive or a negative environment and you have the power to change that environment.

> *"Sports do not build character, they reveal it"*
> **- John Wooden, basketball coach**

TOP PERFORMERS PUT ACTION PLANS INTO ACTION
Positive thoughts inspire positive actions but you must take action to create positive outcomes.

> *"If you set a goal for yourself and you are able to achieve it, you have won your race"*
> **- Dave Scott, triathlete**

AS YOU THINK, YOU BECOME

Your emotional state has a direct impact on your physical state. To generate a success cycle, you must begin by developing an unshakeable self-belief.

"I am the greatest"
- Muhammad Ali, champion boxer

YOU GET OUT WHAT YOU PUT IN

Nothing happens by chance or out with the Laws of the Universe. You get out of life what you put in or you reap what you sow. Winners don't become winners by chance and losers don't become losers by chance.

"The more I practice, the luckier I get"
- Jerry Barber, pro golfer

WINNING EFFORTS RECEIVE WINNING REWARDS

Rewards are always commensurate with effort so if you want to receive a high quality result, you must give a high quality effort.

"Show me a guy who's afraid to look bad, and I'll show you a guy you can beat every time"
- Lou Brock, Major League baseball player

LIKE ATTRACTS LIKE

Positive thoughts lead to positive actions and positive actions lead to positive outcomes. If you generate positive energy, that energy will be returned to you in the form of positive outcomes but generating negative energy can only lead to negative outcomes.

"If you can believe it, the mind can achieve it"
- Ronnie Lott, American football player

WITHOUT CHANGE, NOTHING CHANGES

What you think about, you bring about. We all have the capacity to change our circumstances by changing our thinking.

> *"The key is not the 'will to win' - everybody has that.*
> *It is the will to prepare to win that is important"*
> **- Bobby Knight, basketball coach**

GETTING TO THE TOP MEANS GETTING THINGS IN PERSPECTIVE

Nothing in life has any meaning except for the meaning we give it. Everything is relative to something else so success and failure can only ever be relative to your perspective.

> *"I know I'm never as good or as bad as any single performance"*
> **- Charles Barkley, basketball player**

YOU WIN SOME, YOU LOSE SOME

Everything in life has an opposite. If there was no failure there would be no success and if there were no bad days, there would be no good days.

> *"There's more to boxing than hitting, there's not getting hit, for instance"*
> **- George Foreman, heavyweight boxer**

THE ONLY WAY IS UP...DOWN...UP...

Energy is constantly moving and it moves in continual circles. Where there is setback or injury, there will also be recovery. Your mental attitude has a direct effect on the physical recovery process.

> *"The only way to overcome is to hang in"*
> **- Dan O'Brien, decathlete**

CHAMPIONS RECOGNISE THE CHAMPION WITHIN

You are what you believe you are and your circumstances are an outer reflection of your inner self. Believe in yourself as your best self and you will become your best self.

"Success is about having, excellence is about being. Success is about having money and fame, but excellence is about being the best you can be"
- Mike Ditka, American football player and coach

PERFORMANCE IN ACTION!

Making the leap.

I wryly acknowledged early on in the preparation of this book, that there was an inherent paradox in *writing* about performance - and the act of performing itself.

Let's be honest. Reading the words in these pages can not *give* you the performance enhancement you want in your leisure and sport time, your business or your personal life for that matter...

...so that's precisely why I put together a series of free online performance training videos that will show you exactly how to take these words and understandings, and put them to work for you.

To access these free training videos just visit the website below and you will get instant access to over an hour of personal coaching from me.

I'll also give you details about how YOU can train to become a certified **12 Laws Performance Coach**™

http://www.the12lawsofperformance.co/videos

To your increased performance!

Donald Mac Naughton